I0007308

Amazon ECR User Guide

A catalogue record for this book is available from the Hong Kong Public Libraries.

Published in Hong Kong by Samurai Media Limited.

Email: info@samuraimedia.org

ISBN 9789888408016

Copyright 2018 Amazon Web Services, Inc. and/or its affiliates.
Minor modifications for publication Copyright 2018 Samurai Media Limited.

This book is licensed under the Creative Commons Attribution-ShareAlike 4.0 International Public License.

Background Cover Image by https://www.flickr.com/people/webtreatsetc/

Contents

What Is Amazon Elastic Container Registry?

Amazon Elastic Container Registry (Amazon ECR) is a managed AWS Docker registry service that is secure, scalable, and reliable. Amazon ECR supports private Docker repositories with resource-based permissions using AWS IAM so that specific users or Amazon EC2 instances can access repositories and images. Developers can use the Docker CLI to push, pull, and manage images.

Components of Amazon ECR

Amazon ECR contains the following components:

Registry
An Amazon ECR registry is provided to each AWS account; you can create image repositories in your registry and store images in them. For more information, see Amazon ECR Registries.

Authorization token
Your Docker client needs to authenticate to Amazon ECR registries as an AWS user before it can push and pull images. The AWS CLI get-login command provides you with authentication credentials to pass to Docker. For more information, see Registry Authentication.

Repository
An Amazon ECR image repository contains your Docker images. For more information, see Amazon ECR Repositories.

Repository policy
You can control access to your repositories and the images within them with repository policies. For more information, see Amazon ECR Repository Policies.

Image
You can push and pull Docker images to your repositories. You can use these images locally on your development system, or you can use them in Amazon ECS task definitions. For more information, see Using Amazon ECR Images with Amazon ECS.

How to Get Started with Amazon ECR

To use Amazon ECR, you need to be set up to install the AWS Command Line Interface and Docker. For more information, see Setting Up with Amazon ECR and Docker Basics for Amazon ECR.

After you are set up, you are ready to complete the Getting Started with Amazon ECR tutorial.

Setting Up with Amazon ECR

If you've already signed up for Amazon Web Services (AWS) and have been using Amazon Elastic Container Service (Amazon ECS), you are close to being able to use Amazon ECR. The set up process for the two services is very similar, as Amazon ECR is an extension to Amazon ECS. To use the AWS CLI with Amazon ECR , you must use a version of the AWS CLI that supports the latest Amazon ECR features. If you do not see support for an Amazon ECR feature in the AWS CLI, you should upgrade to the latest version. For more information, see http://aws.amazon.com/cli/.

Complete the following tasks to get set up for Amazon ECR. If you have already completed any of these steps, you may skip them and move on to installing the custom AWS CLI.

1. Sign Up for AWS

2. Create an IAM User

3. Install the AWS CLI

Sign Up for AWS

When you sign up for AWS, your AWS account is automatically signed up for all services, including Amazon ECR. You are charged only for the services that you use.

If you have an AWS account already, skip to the next task. If you don't have an AWS account, use the following procedure to create one.

To create an AWS account

1. Open https://aws.amazon.com/, and then choose **Create an AWS Account**. **Note**
   This might be unavailable in your browser if you previously signed into the AWS Management Console. In that case, choose **Sign in to a different account**, and then choose **Create a new AWS account**.

2. Follow the online instructions.

   Part of the sign-up procedure involves receiving a phone call and entering a PIN using the phone keypad.

Note your AWS account number, because you'll need it for the next task.

Create an IAM User

Services in AWS, such as Amazon ECR, require that you provide credentials when you access them, so that the service can determine whether you have permission to access its resources. The console requires your password. You can create access keys for your AWS account to access the command line interface or API. However, we don't recommend that you access AWS using the credentials for your AWS account; we recommend that you use AWS Identity and Access Management (IAM) instead. Create an IAM user, and then add the user to an IAM group with administrative permissions or grant this user administrative permissions. You can then access AWS using a special URL and the credentials for the IAM user.

If you signed up for AWS but have not created an IAM user for yourself, you can create one using the IAM console.

To create an IAM user for yourself and add the user to an Administrators group

1. Use your AWS account email address and password to sign in as the *AWS account root user* to the IAM console at https://console.aws.amazon.com/iam/. **Note**
   We strongly recommend that you adhere to the best practice of using the **Administrator** IAM user below and securely lock away the root user credentials. Sign in as the root user only to perform a few account and service management tasks.

2. In the navigation pane of the console, choose **Users**, and then choose **Add user**.

3. For **User name**, type **Administrator**.

4. Select the check box next to **AWS Management Console access**, select **Custom password**, and then type the new user's password in the text box. You can optionally select **Require password reset** to force the user to create a new password the next time the user signs in.

5. Choose **Next: Permissions**.

6. On the **Set permissions for user** page, choose **Add user to group**.

7. Choose **Create group**.

8. In the **Create group** dialog box, type **Administrators**.

9. For **Filter**, choose **Job function**.

10. In the policy list, select the check box for **AdministratorAccess**. Then choose **Create group**.

11. Back in the list of groups, select the check box for your new group. Choose **Refresh** if necessary to see the group in the list.

12. Choose **Next: Review** to see the list of group memberships to be added to the new user. When you are ready to proceed, choose **Create user**.

You can use this same process to create more groups and users, and to give your users access to your AWS account resources. To learn about using policies to restrict users' permissions to specific AWS resources, go to Access Management and Example Policies.

To sign in as this new IAM user, sign out of the AWS console, then use the following URL, where *your_aws_account_id* is your AWS account number without the hyphens (for example, if your AWS account number is 1234-5678-9012, your AWS account ID is 123456789012):

```
1 https://your_aws_account_id.signin.aws.amazon.com/console/
```

Enter the IAM user name and password that you just created. When you're signed in, the navigation bar displays *"your_user_name @ your_aws_account_id"*.

If you don't want the URL for your sign-in page to contain your AWS account ID, you can create an account alias. From the IAM dashboard, choose **Create Account Alias** and enter an alias, such as your company name. To sign in after you create an account alias, use the following URL:

```
1 https://your_account_alias.signin.aws.amazon.com/console/
```

To verify the sign-in link for IAM users for your account, open the IAM console and check under **IAM users sign-in link** on the dashboard.

For more information about IAM, see the AWS Identity and Access Management User Guide.

Install the AWS CLI

You can use the AWS command line tools to issue commands at your system's command line to perform Amazon ECS and AWS tasks; this can be faster and more convenient than using the console. The command line tools are also useful if you want to build scripts that perform AWS tasks.

To use the AWS CLI with Amazon ECR, install the latest AWS CLI version (Amazon ECR functionality is available in the AWS CLI starting with version 1.9.15). You can check your AWS CLI version with the aws --version command. For information about installing the AWS CLI or upgrading it to the latest version, see Installing the AWS Command Line Interface in the *AWS Command Line Interface User Guide*.

Install Docker

To use the Docker CLI with Amazon ECR, you must first install Docker on your system. For information about installing Docker and getting familiar with the tools, see Docker Basics for Amazon ECR.

Docker Basics for Amazon ECR

Docker is a technology that allows you to build, run, test, and deploy distributed applications that are based on Linux containers. Amazon ECR is a managed AWS Docker registry service. Customers can use the familiar Docker CLI to push, pull, and manage images. For Amazon ECR product details, featured customer case studies, and FAQs, see the Amazon Elastic Container Registry product detail pages.

The documentation in this guide assumes that readers possess a basic understanding of what Docker is and how it works. For more information about Docker, see What is Docker? and the Docker overview.

Topics

- Installing Docker
- Create a Docker Image
- (Optional) Push your image to Amazon Elastic Container Registry
- Next Steps

Installing Docker

Note
If you already have Docker installed, skip to Create a Docker Image.

Docker is available on many different operating systems, including most modern Linux distributions, like Ubuntu, and even Mac OSX and Windows. For more information about how to install Docker on your particular operating system, go to the Docker installation guide.

You don't even need a local development system to use Docker. If you are using Amazon EC2 already, you can launch an Amazon Linux instance and install Docker to get started.

To install Docker on an Amazon Linux instance

1. Launch an instance with the Amazon Linux AMI. For more information, see Launching an Instance in the *Amazon EC2 User Guide for Linux Instances*.

2. Connect to your instance. For more information, see Connect to Your Linux Instance in the *Amazon EC2 User Guide for Linux Instances*.

3. Update the installed packages and package cache on your instance.

```
1 sudo yum update -y
```

4. Install the most recent Docker Community Edition package.

```
1 sudo yum install -y docker
```

5. Start the Docker service.

```
1 sudo service docker start
```

6. Add the ec2-user to the docker group so you can execute Docker commands without using sudo.

```
1 sudo usermod -a -G docker ec2-user
```

7. Log out and log back in again to pick up the new docker group permissions. You can accomplish this by closing your current SSH terminal window and reconnecting to your instance in a new one. Your new SSH session will have the appropriate docker group permissions.

8. Verify that the ec2-user can run Docker commands without sudo.

```
1 docker info
```

Note

In some cases, you may need to reboot your instance to provide permissions for the `ec2-user` to access the Docker daemon. Try rebooting your instance if you see the following error:

```
1 Cannot connect to the Docker daemon. Is the docker daemon running on this host?
```

Create a Docker Image

In this section, you create a Docker image of a simple web application, and test it on your local system or EC2 instance, and then push the image to a container registry (such as Amazon ECR or Docker Hub) so you can use it in an ECS task definition.

To create a Docker image of a simple web application

1. Create a file called `Dockerfile`. A Dockerfile is a manifest that describes the base image to use for your Docker image and what you want installed and running on it. For more information about Dockerfiles, go to the Dockerfile Reference.

```
1 touch Dockerfile
```

2. Edit the `Dockerfile` you just created and add the following content.

```
1 FROM ubuntu:12.04
2
3 # Install dependencies
4 RUN apt-get update -y
5 RUN apt-get install -y apache2
6
7 # Install apache and write hello world message
8 RUN echo "Hello World!" > /var/www/index.html
9
10 # Configure apache
11 RUN a2enmod rewrite
12 RUN chown -R www-data:www-data /var/www
13 ENV APACHE_RUN_USER www-data
14 ENV APACHE_RUN_GROUP www-data
15 ENV APACHE_LOG_DIR /var/log/apache2
16
17 EXPOSE 80
18
19 CMD ["/usr/sbin/apache2", "-D", "FOREGROUND"]
```

This Dockerfile uses the Ubuntu 12.04 image. The `RUN` instructions update the package caches, install some software packages for the web server, and then write the "Hello World!" content to the web server's document root. The `EXPOSE` instruction exposes port 80 on the container, and the `CMD` instruction starts the web server.

3. Build the Docker image from your Dockerfile. **Note**
Some versions of Docker may require the full path to your Dockerfile in the following command, instead of the relative path shown below.

```
1 docker build -t hello-world .
```

4. Run docker images to verify that the image was created correctly.

```
1 docker images --filter reference=hello-world
```

Output:

```
1 REPOSITORY          TAG           IMAGE ID          CREATED           SIZE
2 hello-world         latest        e9ffedc8c286      4 minutes ago     258MB
```

5. Run the newly built image. The `-p 80:80` option maps the exposed port 80 on the container to port 80 on the host system. For more information about docker run, go to the Docker run reference.

```
1 docker run -p 80:80 hello-world
```

Note
Output from the Apache web server is displayed in the terminal window. You can ignore the "Could not reliably determine the server's fully qualified domain name" message.

1. Open a browser and point to the server that is running Docker and hosting your container.

   - If you are using an EC2 instance, this is the **Public DNS** value for the server, which is the same address you use to connect to the instance with SSH. Make sure that the security group for your instance allows inbound traffic on port 80.

   - If you are running Docker locally, point your browser to http://localhost/.

   - If you are using docker-machine on a Windows or Mac computer, find the IP address of the VirtualBox VM that is hosting Docker with the docker-machine ip command, substituting *machine-name* with the name of the docker machine you are using.

   ```
   1 docker-machine ip machine-name
   ```

   You should see a web page with your "Hello World!" statement.

2. Stop the Docker container by typing **Ctrl + c**.

(Optional) Push your image to Amazon Elastic Container Registry

Amazon ECR is a managed AWS Docker registry service. Customers can use the familiar Docker CLI to push, pull, and manage images. For Amazon ECR product details, featured customer case studies, and FAQs, see the Amazon Elastic Container Registry product detail pages.

Note
This section requires the AWS CLI. If you do not have the AWS CLI installed on your system, see Installing the AWS Command Line Interface in the *AWS Command Line Interface User Guide*.

To tag your image and push it to Amazon ECR

1. Create an Amazon ECR repository to store your `hello-world` image. Note the `repositoryUri` in the output.

   ```
   1 aws ecr create-repository --repository-name hello-world
   ```

   Output:

   ```
   1 {
   2     "repository": {
   3         "registryId": "aws_account_id",
   4         "repositoryName": "hello-world",
   5         "repositoryArn": "arn:aws:ecr:us-east-1:aws_account_id:repository/hello-world",
   6         "createdAt": 1505337806.0,
   7         "repositoryUri": "aws_account_id.dkr.ecr.us-east-1.amazonaws.com/hello-world"
   8     }
   9 }
   ```

2. Tag the `hello-world` image with the `repositoryUri` value from the previous step.

```
1 docker tag hello-world aws_account_id.dkr.ecr.us-east-1.amazonaws.com/hello-world
```

3. Run the aws ecr get-login --no-include-email command to get the docker login authentication command string for your registry. **Note**
   The get-login command is available in the AWS CLI starting with version 1.9.15; however, we recommend version 1.11.91 or later for recent versions of Docker (17.06 or later). You can check your AWS CLI version with the aws --version command. If you are using Docker version 17.06 or later, include the `--no-include-email` option after `get-login`. If you receive an `Unknown options: --no-include-email` error, install the latest version of the AWS CLI. For more information, see Installing the AWS Command Line Interface in the *AWS Command Line Interface User Guide*.

```
1 aws ecr get-login --no-include-email
```

4. Run the docker login command that was returned in the previous step. This command provides an authorization token that is valid for 12 hours. **Important**
   When you execute this docker login command, the command string can be visible to other users on your system in a process list (ps -e) display. Because the docker login command contains authentication credentials, there is a risk that other users on your system could view them this way and use them to gain push and pull access to your repositories. If you are not on a secure system, you should consider this risk and log in interactively by omitting the `-p password` option, and then entering the password when prompted.

5. Push the image to Amazon ECR with the `repositoryUri` value from the earlier step.

```
1 docker push aws_account_id.dkr.ecr.us-east-1.amazonaws.com/hello-world
```

Next Steps

When you are done experimenting with your Amazon ECR image, you can delete the repository so you are not charged for image storage.

Note
This section requires the AWS CLI. If you do not have the AWS CLI installed on your system, see Installing the AWS Command Line Interface in the *AWS Command Line Interface User Guide*.

```
1 aws ecr delete-repository --repository-name hello-world --force
```

Getting Started with Amazon ECR

Get started with Amazon Elastic Container Registry (Amazon ECR) by creating a repository in the Amazon ECS console. The Amazon ECR first run wizard guides you through the process to get started with Amazon ECR.

Important

Before you begin, be sure that you've completed the steps in Setting Up with Amazon ECR.

Configure repository

A repository is where you store Docker images in Amazon ECR. Every time you push or pull an image from Amazon ECR, you specify the registry and repository location to tell Docker where to push the image to or where to pull it from.

1. Open the Amazon ECS console repositories page at https://console.aws.amazon.com/ecs/home# /repositories.

2. For **Repository name**, enter a unique name for your repository and choose **Next step**.

Build, tag, and push Docker image

In this section of the wizard, you use the Docker CLI to tag an existing local image (that you have built from a Dockerfile or pulled from another registry, such as Docker Hub) and then push the tagged image to your Amazon ECR registry.

1. Retrieve the docker login command that you can use to authenticate your Docker client to your registry by pasting the aws ecr get-login command from the console into a terminal window. **Note**
The get-login command is available in the AWS CLI starting with version 1.9.15; however, we recommend version 1.11.91 or later for recent versions of Docker (17.06 or later). You can check your AWS CLI version with the aws --version command. If you are using Docker version 17.06 or later, include the `--no-include -email` option after `get-login`. If you receive an `Unknown options: --no-include-email` error, install the latest version of the AWS CLI. For more information, see Installing the AWS Command Line Interface in the *AWS Command Line Interface User Guide.*

2. Run the docker login command that was returned in the previous step. This command provides an authorization token that is valid for 12 hours. **Important**
When you execute this docker login command, the command string can be visible to other users on your system in a process list (ps -e) display. Because the docker login command contains authentication credentials, there is a risk that other users on your system could view them this way and use them to gain push and pull access to your repositories. If you are not on a secure system, you should consider this risk and log in interactively by omitting the `-p password` option, and then entering the password when prompted.

3. (Optional) If you have a Dockerfile for the image to push, build the image and tag it for your new repository by pasting the docker build command from the console into a terminal window. Make sure you are in the same directory as your Dockerfile.

4. Tag the image for your ECR registry and your new repository by pasting the docker tag command from the console into a terminal window. The console command assumes that your image was built from a Dockerfile in the previous step; if you did not build your image from a Dockerfile, replace the first instance of `repository:latest` with the image ID or image name of your local image to push.

5. Push the newly tagged image to your ECR repository by pasting the docker push command into a terminal window.

6. Choose **Done**.

Amazon ECR Registries

You can use Amazon ECR registries to host your images in a highly available and scalable architecture, allowing you to deploy containers reliably for your applications. You can use your registry to manage image repositories and Docker images. Each AWS account is provided with a single (default) Amazon ECR registry.

Registry Concepts

- The URL for your default registry is `https://``aws_account_id.dkr.ecr.region.amazonaws.com`.
- By default, you have read and write access to the repositories and images you create in your default registry.
- You must authenticate your Docker client to a registry so that you can use the docker push and docker pull commands to push and pull images to and from the repositories in that registry. For more information, see Registry Authentication.
- Repositories can be controlled with both IAM user access policies and repository policies.

Registry Authentication

You can use the AWS Management Console, the AWS CLI, or the AWS SDKs to create and manage repositories, and to perform some actions on images, such as listing or deleting them. These clients use standard AWS authentication methods. Although technically you can use the Amazon ECR API to push and pull images, you are much more likely to use Docker CLI (or a language-specific Docker library) for these purposes.

Because the Docker CLI does not support the standard AWS authentication methods, you must authenticate your Docker client another way so that Amazon ECR knows who is requesting to push or pull an image. If you are using the Docker CLI, then use the docker login command to authenticate to an Amazon ECR registry with an authorization token that is provided by Amazon ECR and is valid for 12 hours. The GetAuthorizationToken API operation provides a base64-encoded authorization token that contains a user name (`AWS`) and a password that you can decode and use in a docker login command. However, a much simpler get-login command (which retrieves the token, decodes it, and converts it to a docker login command for you) is available in the AWS CLI.

To authenticate Docker to an Amazon ECR registry with get-login Note
The get-login command is available in the AWS CLI starting with version 1.9.15; however, we recommend version 1.11.91 or later for recent versions of Docker (17.06 or later). You can check your AWS CLI version with the aws --version command.

1. Run the aws ecr get-login command. The example below is for the default registry associated with the account making the request. To access other account registries, use the `--registry-ids aws_account_id` option. For more information, see get-login in the *AWS CLI Command Reference*.

```
1 aws ecr get-login --no-include-email
```

Output:

```
1 docker login -u AWS -p password https://aws_account_id.dkr.ecr.us-east-1.amazonaws.com
```

Important
If you receive an `Unknown options: --no-include-email` error, install the latest version of the AWS CLI. For more information, see Installing the AWS Command Line Interface in the *AWS Command Line Interface User Guide*.

The resulting output is a docker login command that you use to authenticate your Docker client to your Amazon ECR registry.

1. Copy and paste the docker login command into a terminal to authenticate your Docker CLI to the registry. This command provides an authorization token that is valid for the specified registry for 12 hours. **Note** If you are using Windows PowerShell, copying and pasting long strings like this does not work. Use the following command instead.

```
1 Invoke-Expression -Command (aws ecr get-login --no-include-email)
```

Important

When you execute this docker login command, the command string can be visible to other users on your system in a process list (ps -e) display. Because the docker login command contains authentication credentials, there is a risk that other users on your system could view them this way and use them to gain push and pull access to your repositories. If you are not on a secure system, you should consider this risk and log in interactively by omitting the `-p password` option, and then entering the password when prompted.

HTTP API Authentication

Amazon ECR supports the Docker Registry HTTP API. However, because Amazon ECR is a private registry, you must provide an authorization token with every HTTP request. You can add an HTTP authorization header using the -H option for curl and pass the authorization token provided by the get-authorization-token AWS CLI command.

To authenticate with the Amazon ECR HTTP API

1. Retrieve an authorization token with the AWS CLI and set it to an environment variable.

```
1 TOKEN=$(aws ecr get-authorization-token --output text --query authorizationData[].
    authorizationToken)
```

2. Pass the $TOKEN variable to the -H option of curl to authenticate to the API. For example, the following command lists the image tags in an Amazon ECR repository. For more information, see the Docker Registry HTTP API reference documentation.

```
1 curl -i -H "Authorization: Basic $TOKEN" https://012345678910.dkr.ecr.us-east-1.amazonaws.
    com/v2/amazonlinux/tags/list
```

Output:

```
1 HTTP/1.1 200 OK
2 Content-Type: text/plain; charset=utf-8
3 Date: Thu, 04 Jan 2018 16:06:59 GMT
4 Docker-Distribution-Api-Version: registry/2.0
5 Content-Length: 50
6 Connection: keep-alive
7
8 {"name":"amazonlinux","tags":["2017.09","latest"]}
```

Amazon ECR Repositories

Amazon ECR provides API operations to create, monitor, and delete repositories and set repository permissions that control who can access them. You can perform the same actions in the **Repositories** section of the Amazon ECS console. Amazon ECR also integrates with the Docker CLI allowing you to push and pull images from your development environments to your repositories.

Topics

- Repository Concepts
- Creating a Repository
- Viewing Repository Information
- Deleting a Repository
- Amazon ECR Repository Policies

Repository Concepts

- By default, your account has read and write access to the repositories in your default registry (`aws_account_id.dkr.ecr.region.amazonaws.com`). However, IAM users require permissions to make calls to the Amazon ECR APIs and to push or pull images from your repositories. Amazon ECR provides several managed policies to control user access at varying levels; for more information, see Amazon ECR Managed Policies.
- Repositories can be controlled with both IAM user access policies and repository policies. For more information, see Amazon ECR Repository Policies.
- Repository names can support namespaces, which you can use to group similar repositories. For example if there are several teams using the same registry, Team A could use the `team-a` namespace while Team B uses the `team-b` namespace. Each team could have their own image called `web-app`, but because they are each prefaced with the team namespace, the two images can be used simultaneously without interference. Team A's image would be called `team-a/web-app`, while Team B's image would be called `team-b/web-app`.

Creating a Repository

Before you can push your Docker images to Amazon ECR, you need to create a repository to store them in. You can create Amazon ECR repositories with the AWS Management Console, or with the AWS CLI and AWS SDKs.

To create a repository

1. Open the Amazon ECS console at https://console.aws.amazon.com/ecs/.

2. From the navigation bar, choose the region to create your repository in.

3. In the navigation pane, choose **Repositories**.

4. On the **Repositories** page, choose **Create repository**.

5. For **Repository name**, enter a unique name for your repository and choose **Next step**.

6. (Optional) On the **Build, tag, and push Docker image** page, complete the following steps to push an image to your new repository. If you do not want to push an image at this time, you can choose **Done** to finish.

   1. Retrieve the docker login command that you can use to authenticate your Docker client to your registry by pasting the aws ecr get-login command from the console into a terminal window. **Note** The get-login command is available in the AWS CLI starting with version 1.9.15; however, we recommend version 1.11.91 or later for recent versions of Docker (17.06 or later). You can check your AWS CLI version with the aws --version command. If you are using Docker version 17.06 or later, include the `--no-include-email` option after `get-login`. If you receive an `Unknown options : --no-include-email` error, install the latest version of the AWS CLI. For more information, see Installing the AWS Command Line Interface in the *AWS Command Line Interface User Guide*.

   2. Run the docker login command that was returned in the previous step. This command provides an authorization token that is valid for 12 hours. **Important** When you execute this docker login command, the command string can be visible to other users on your system in a process list (ps -e) display. Because the docker login command contains authentication credentials, there is a risk that other users on your system could view them this way and use them to gain push and pull access to your repositories. If you are not on a secure system, you should consider this risk and log in interactively by omitting the `-p password` option, and then entering the password when prompted.

   3. (Optional) If you have a Dockerfile for the image to push, build the image and tag it for your new repository by pasting the docker build command from the console into a terminal window. Make sure you are in the same directory as your Dockerfile.

   4. Tag the image for your ECR registry and your new repository by pasting the docker tag command from the console into a terminal window. The console command assumes that your image was built from a Dockerfile in the previous step; if you did not build your image from a Dockerfile, replace the first instance of `repository:latest` with the image ID or image name of your local image to push.

   5. Push the newly tagged image to your ECR repository by pasting the docker push command into a terminal window.

   6. Choose **Done**.

Viewing Repository Information

After you have created a repository, you can view its information in the AWS Management Console. You can see which images are stored in a repository, whether or not an image is tagged and what the tags for the image are, the SHA digest for the images, the size of the images in MiB, and when the image was pushed to the repository.

Note
Beginning with Docker version 1.9, the Docker client compresses image layers before pushing them to a V2 Docker registry. The output of the docker images command shows the uncompressed image size, so it may return a larger image size than the image sizes shown in the AWS Management Console.

You can also view the repository policies that are applied to the repository.

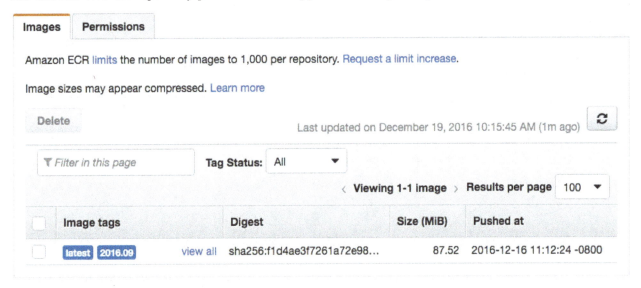

To view repository information

1. Open the Amazon ECS console at https://console.aws.amazon.com/ecs/.

2. From the navigation bar, choose the region that contains the repository to view.

3. In the navigation pane, choose **Repositories**.

4. On the **Repositories** page, choose the repository to view.

5. On the **All repositories : *repository_name*** page, choose the tab which corresponds to the information you would like to view.

   - Choose the **Images** tab to view information about the images in the repository. If there are untagged images that you would like to delete, you can select the box to the left of the repositories to delete and choose **Delete**. For more information, see Deleting an Image.
   - Choose the **Permissions** tab to view the repository policies that are applied to the repository. For more information, see Amazon ECR Repository Policies.

Deleting a Repository

If you are done using a repository, you can delete it. When you delete a repository in the AWS Management Console, all of the images contained in the repository are also deleted; this cannot be undone.

To delete a repository

1. Open the Amazon ECS console at https://console.aws.amazon.com/ecs/.

2. From the navigation bar, choose the region that contains the repository to delete.

3. In the navigation pane, choose **Repositories**.

4. On the **Repositories** page, select the box to the left of the repositories to delete and choose **Delete repository**.

5. In the **Delete repository** window, verify that the selected repositories should be deleted and choose **Delete**. **Important**
   Any images in the selected repositories is also deleted.

Amazon ECR Repository Policies

Amazon ECR uses resource-based permissions to control access. Resource-based permissions let you specify who has access to a repository and what actions they can perform on it. By default, only the repository owner has access to a repository. You can apply a policy document that allows others to access your repository.

Important
Amazon ECR users require permissions to call `ecr:GetAuthorizationToken` before they can authenticate to a registry and push or pull any images from any Amazon ECR repository. Amazon ECR provides several managed policies to control user access at varying levels; for more information, see Amazon ECR Managed Policies.

Topics

- Setting a Repository Policy Statement
- Deleting a Repository Policy Statement
- Amazon ECR Repository Policy Examples

Setting a Repository Policy Statement

You can create and set an access policy statement for your repositories in the AWS Management Console by following the steps below. You can create multiple policy statements per repository.

Important
Amazon ECR users require permissions to call `ecr:GetAuthorizationToken` before they can authenticate to a registry and push or pull any images from any Amazon ECR repository. Amazon ECR provides several managed policies to control user access at varying levels; for more information, see Amazon ECR Managed Policies.

To set a repository policy statement

1. Open the Amazon ECS console at https://console.aws.amazon.com/ecs/.

2. From the navigation bar, choose the region that contains the repository to set a policy statement on.

3. In the navigation pane, choose **Repositories**.

4. On the **Repositories** page, choose the repository to set a policy statement on.

5. On the **All repositories:** *repository_name* page, choose **Permissions**, **Add**.

6. For **Sid**, enter a description for what your policy statement does.

7. For **Effect**, choose whether the policy statement should allow access or deny it.

8. For **Principal**, choose the scope of users to apply the policy statement to.

   - You can apply the statement to all authenticated AWS users by selecting the **Everybody** check box.
   - You can apply the statement to all users under specific AWS accounts by listing those account numbers (for example, 111122223333) in the **AWS account number(s)** field.
   - You can apply the statement to roles or users under your AWS account by checking the roles or users under the **All IAM entities** list and choosing **»** **Add** to move them to the **Selected IAM entities** list. **Note**
     For more complicated repository policies that are not currently supported in the AWS Management Console, you can apply the policy with the set-repository-policy AWS CLI command.

9. For **Action**, choose the scope of the Amazon ECR API operations that the policy statement should apply to. You can choose individual API operations, or you can choose from the preset task-based options.

   - **All actions** sets the scope to all Amazon ECR API operations.
   - **Push/Pull actions** sets the scope to Amazon ECR API operations required to push or pull images in this repository with the Docker CLI.
   - **Pull only actions** sets the scope to Amazon ECR API operations required only to pull images from this repository with the Docker CLI.

10. When you are finished, choose **Save** to set the policy. **Important**
    Amazon ECR users require permissions to call `ecr:GetAuthorizationToken` before they can authenticate to a registry and push or pull any images from any Amazon ECR repository. Amazon ECR provides several managed policies to control user access at varying levels; for more information, see Amazon ECR Managed Policies.

Deleting a Repository Policy Statement

If you no longer want an existing repository policy statement to apply to a repository, you can delete it.

To delete a repository policy statement

1. Open the Amazon ECS console at https://console.aws.amazon.com/ecs/.

2. From the navigation bar, choose the region that contains the repository to delete a policy statement from.

3. In the navigation pane, choose **Repositories**.

4. On the **Repositories** page, choose the repository to delete a policy statement from.

5. On the **All repositories :** *repository_name* page, choose the **Permissions** tab.

6. In the **Permission statements** list, expand the policy statement to delete and choose **Remove** at the bottom of the expanded statement.

Amazon ECR Repository Policy Examples

The following examples show policy statements that you could use to control the permissions that users have to Amazon ECR repositories.

Important

Amazon ECR users require permissions to call `ecr:GetAuthorizationToken` before they can authenticate to a registry and push or pull any images from any Amazon ECR repository. Amazon ECR provides several managed policies to control user access at varying levels; for more information, see Amazon ECR Managed Policies.

Topics

- Example: Allow IAM Users Within Your Account
- Example: Allow Other Accounts
- Example: Deny All

Example: Allow IAM Users Within Your Account

The following repository policy allows IAM users within your account to push and pull images.

```
1  {
2    "Version": "2008-10-17",
3    "Statement": [
4      {
5        "Sid": "AllowPushPull",
6        "Effect": "Allow",
7        "Principal": {
8          "AWS": [
9            "arn:aws:iam::aws_account_id:user/push-pull-user-1",
10           "arn:aws:iam::aws_account_id:user/push-pull-user-2"
11         ]
12       },
13       "Action": [
14         "ecr:GetDownloadUrlForLayer",
15         "ecr:BatchGetImage",
16         "ecr:BatchCheckLayerAvailability",
17         "ecr:PutImage",
18         "ecr:InitiateLayerUpload",
19         "ecr:UploadLayerPart",
20         "ecr:CompleteLayerUpload"
21       ]
22     }
23   ]
24 }
```

Example: Allow Other Accounts

The following repository policy allows a specific account to push images.

```
1  {
2    "Version": "2008-10-17",
3    "Statement": [
4      {
5        "Sid": "AllowCrossAccountPush",
```

```
6        "Effect": "Allow",
7        "Principal": {
8          "AWS": "arn:aws:iam::aws_account_id:root"
9        },
10       "Action": [
11         "ecr:GetDownloadUrlForLayer",
12         "ecr:BatchCheckLayerAvailability",
13         "ecr:PutImage",
14         "ecr:InitiateLayerUpload",
15         "ecr:UploadLayerPart",
16         "ecr:CompleteLayerUpload"
17       ]
18     }
19   ]
20 }
```

The following repository policy allows all AWS accounts to pull images.

```
1  {
2    "Version": "2008-10-17",
3    "Statement": [
4      {
5        "Sid": "AllowPull",
6        "Effect": "Allow",
7        "Principal": "*",
8        "Action": [
9          "ecr:GetDownloadUrlForLayer",
10         "ecr:BatchGetImage",
11         "ecr:BatchCheckLayerAvailability"
12       ]
13     }
14   ]
15 }
```

The following repository policy allows some IAM users to pull images (*pull-user-1* and *pull-user-2*) while providing full access to another (*admin-user*).

Note

For more complicated repository policies that are not currently supported in the AWS Management Console, you can apply the policy with the set-repository-policy AWS CLI command.

```
1  {
2    "Version": "2008-10-17",
3    "Statement": [
4      {
5        "Sid": "AllowPull",
6        "Effect": "Allow",
7        "Principal": {
8          "AWS": [
9            "arn:aws:iam::aws_account_id:user/pull-user-1",
10           "arn:aws:iam::aws_account_id:user/pull-user-2"
11         ]
12       },
13       "Action": [
14         "ecr:GetDownloadUrlForLayer",
15         "ecr:BatchGetImage",
```

```
16          "ecr:BatchCheckLayerAvailability"
17        ]
18      },
19      {
20        "Sid": "AllowAll",
21        "Effect": "Allow",
22        "Principal": {
23          "AWS": "arn:aws:iam::aws_account_id:user/admin-user"
24        },
25        "Action": [
26          "ecr:*"
27        ]
28      }
29    ]
30  }
```

Example: Deny All

The following repository policy denies all users the ability to pull images.

```
1   {
2     "Version": "2008-10-17",
3     "Statement": [
4       {
5         "Sid": "DenyPull",
6         "Effect": "Deny",
7         "Principal": "*",
8         "Action": [
9           "ecr:GetDownloadUrlForLayer",
10          "ecr:BatchGetImage",
11          "ecr:BatchCheckLayerAvailability"
12        ]
13      }
14    ]
15  }
```

Images

Amazon ECR stores Docker images in image repositories. You can use the Docker CLI to push and pull images from your repositories.

Important
Amazon ECR users require permissions to call `ecr:GetAuthorizationToken` before they can authenticate to a registry and push or pull any images from any Amazon ECR repository. Amazon ECR provides several managed policies to control user access at varying levels; for more information, see Amazon ECR Managed Policies.

Topics
- Pushing an Image
- Retagging an Image with the AWS CLI
- Retagging an Image with the AWS Tools for Windows PowerShell
- Pulling an Image
- Container Image Manifest Formats
- Using Amazon ECR Images with Amazon ECS
- Deleting an Image
- Amazon Linux Container Image
- Amazon ECR Lifecycle Policies

Pushing an Image

If you have a Docker image available in your development environment, you can push it to an Amazon ECR repository with the docker push command.

Important

Amazon ECR users require permissions to call `ecr:GetAuthorizationToken` before they can authenticate to a registry and push or pull any images from any Amazon ECR repository. Amazon ECR provides several managed policies to control user access at varying levels; for more information, see Amazon ECR Managed Policies.

To push a Docker image to an Amazon ECR repository

1. Authenticate your Docker client to the Amazon ECR registry you intend to push your image to. Authentication tokens must be obtained for each registry used, and the tokens are valid for 12 hours. For more information, see Registry Authentication.

2. If your image repository does not exist in the registry you intend to push to yet, create it. For more information, see Creating a Repository.

3. Identify the image to push. Run the docker images command to list the images on your system.

```
1 docker images
```

   You can identify an image with the *repository:tag* or the image ID in the resulting command output.

4. Tag your image with the Amazon ECR registry, repository, and optional image tag name combination to use. The registry format is `aws_account_id.dkr.ecr.region.amazonaws.com`. The repository name should match the repository that you created for your image. If you omit the image tag, we assume the tag is `latest`.

   The following example tags an image with the ID *e9ae3c220b23* as `aws_account_id.dkr.ecr.region.amazonaws.com``/my-web-app`.

```
1 docker tag e9ae3c220b23 aws_account_id.dkr.ecr.region.amazonaws.com/my-web-app
```

5. Push the image using the docker push command.

```
1 docker push aws_account_id.dkr.ecr.region.amazonaws.com/my-web-app
```

6. (Optional) Apply any additional tags to your image and push those tags to Amazon ECR by repeating Step 4 and Step 5. You can apply up to 100 tags per image in Amazon ECR.

Retagging an Image with the AWS CLI

With Docker Image Manifest V2 Schema 2 images, you can use the `--image-tag` option of the put-image command to retag an existing image, without pulling or pushing the image with Docker. For larger images, this process saves a considerable amount of network bandwidth and time required to retag an image.

Note
This procedure does not work for Windows clients because of the way the AWS CLI output text is interpreted by the shell. To retag an image on Windows clients, see Retagging an Image with the AWS Tools for Windows PowerShell.

To retag an image with the AWS CLI

1. Use the batch-get-image command to get the image manifest for the image to retag and write it to an environment variable. In this example, the manifest for an image with the tag, *latest*, in the repository, *amazonlinux*, is written to the environment variable, *MANIFEST*.

```
1 MANIFEST=$(aws ecr batch-get-image --repository-name amazonlinux --image-ids imageTag=
    latest --query images[].imageManifest --output text)
```

2. Use the `--image-tag` option of the put-image command to put the image manifest to Amazon ECR with a new tag. In this example, the image is tagged as *2017.03*. **Note**
If the `--image-tag` option is not available in your version of the AWS CLI, upgrade to the latest version. For more information, see Installing the AWS Command Line Interface in the *AWS Command Line Interface User Guide*.

```
1 aws ecr put-image --repository-name amazonlinux --image-tag 2017.03 --image-manifest "
    $MANIFEST"
```

3. Verify that your new image tag is attached to your image. In the output below, the image has the tags `latest` and `2017.03`.

```
1 aws ecr describe-images --repository-name amazonlinux
```

Output:

```
1  {
2      "imageDetails": [
3          {
4              "imageSizeInBytes": 98755613,
5              "imageDigest": "sha256:8
                  d00af8f076eb15a33019c2a3e7f1f655375681c4e5be157a2685dfe6f247227",
6              "imageTags": [
7                  "latest",
8                  "2017.03"
9              ],
10             "registryId": "aws_account_id",
11             "repositoryName": "amazonlinux",
12             "imagePushedAt": 1499287667.0
13         }
14     ]
15 }
```

Retagging an Image with the AWS Tools for Windows PowerShell

With Docker Image Manifest V2 Schema 2 images, you can use the `-ImageTag` option of the AWS Tools for Windows PowerShell Get-ECRImage cmdlet to retag an existing image, without pulling or pushing the image with Docker. For larger images, this process saves a considerable amount of network bandwidth and time required to retag an image.

To retag an image with the AWS Tools for Windows PowerShell

1. Use the Get-ECRImageBatch cmdlet to get the description of the image to retag and write it to an environment variable. In this example, an image with the tag, *latest*, in the repository, *amazonlinux*, is written to the environment variable, *$Image*. **Note**
   If you don't have the Get-ECRImageBatch cmdlet available on your system, see Setting up the AWS Tools for Windows PowerShell in the *AWS Tools for Windows PowerShell User Guide*.

```
1 $Image = Get-ECRImageBatch -ImageId @{ imageTag="latest" } -RepositoryName amazonlinux
```

2. Write the manifest of the image to the *$Manifest* environment variable.

```
1 $Manifest = $Image.Images[0].ImageManifest
```

3. Use the `-ImageTag` option of the Write-ECRImage cmdlet to put the image manifest to Amazon ECR with a new tag. In this example, the image is tagged as *2017.09*.

```
1 Write-ECRImage -RepositoryName amazonlinux -ImageManifest $Manifest -ImageTag 2017.09
```

4. Verify that your new image tag is attached to your image. In the output below, the image has the tags `latest` and `2017.09`.

```
1 Get-ECRImage -RepositoryName amazonlinux
```

Output:

```
1 ImageDigest                                                              ImageTag
2 -----------                                                              --------
3 sha256:359b948ea8866817e94765822787cd482279eed0c17bc674a7707f4256d5d497 latest
4 sha256:359b948ea8866817e94765822787cd482279eed0c17bc674a7707f4256d5d497 2017.09
```

Pulling an Image

If you would like to run a Docker image that is available in Amazon ECR (either in your default registry or from a registry associated with another AWS account), you can pull it to your local environment with the docker pull command. If you want to use an Amazon ECR image in an Amazon ECS task definition, see Using Amazon ECR Images with Amazon ECS.

Important

Amazon ECR users require permissions to call `ecr:GetAuthorizationToken` before they can authenticate to a registry and push or pull any images from any Amazon ECR repository. Amazon ECR provides several managed policies to control user access at varying levels; for more information, see Amazon ECR Managed Policies.

To pull a Docker image from an Amazon ECR repository

1. Authenticate your Docker client to the Amazon ECR registry that you intend to pull your image from. Authentication tokens must be obtained for each registry used, and the tokens are valid for 12 hours. For more information, see Registry Authentication.

2. (Optional) Identify the image to pull.

   - You can list the repositories in a registry with the aws ecr describe-repositories command.

   ```
   1 aws ecr describe-repositories
   ```

   The example registry above has a repository called `amazonlinux`.

   - You can describe the images within a repository with the aws ecr describe-images command.

   ```
   1 aws ecr describe-images --repository-name amazonlinux
   ```

   The example repository above has an image tagged as `latest` and `2016.09`, with the image digest `sha256:f1d4ae3f7261a72e98c6ebefe9985cf10a0ea5bd762585a43e0700ed99863807`.

3. Pull the image using the docker pull command. The image name format should be **registry/repository [:tag]** to pull by tag, or **registry/repository[@digest]** to pull by digest.

   ```
   1 docker pull aws_account_id.dkr.ecr.us-west-2.amazonaws.com/amazonlinux:latest
   ```

Important

If you receive a `repository-url not found: does not exist or no pull access` error, you may need to authenticate your Docker client with Amazon ECR. For more information, see Registry Authentication.

Container Image Manifest Formats

Amazon ECR supports the following container image manifest formats:

- Docker Image Manifest V2 Schema 1 (used with Docker version 1.9 and older)
- Docker Image Manifest V2 Schema 2 (used with Docker version 1.10 and newer)
- Open Container Initiative (OCI) Specifications (v1.0 and up)

Support for Docker Image Manifest V2 Schema 2 provides the following functionality:

- The ability to use multiple tags per image.
- Support for storing Windows container images. For more information, see Pushing Windows Images to Amazon ECR in the *Amazon Elastic Container Service Developer Guide*.

Amazon ECR Image Manifest Conversion

When you push and pull images to and from Amazon ECR, your container engine client (for example, Docker) communicates with the registry to agree on a manifest format that is understood by the client and the registry to use for the image.

When you push an image to Amazon ECR with Docker version 1.9 or older, the image manifest format is stored as Docker Image Manifest V2 Schema 1. When you push an image to Amazon ECR with Docker version 1.10 or newer, the image manifest format is stored as Docker Image Manifest V2 Schema 2.

When you pull an image from Amazon ECR *by tag*, Amazon ECR returns the image manifest format that is stored in the repository, but only if that format is understood by the client. If the stored image manifest format is not understood by the client (for example, if a Docker 1.9 client requests an image manifest that is stored as Docker Image Manifest V2 Schema 2), Amazon ECR converts the image manifest into a format that is understood by the client (in this case, Docker Image Manifest V2 Schema 1). The table below describes the available conversions supported by Amazon ECR when an image is pulled *by tag*:

Schema requested by client	Pushed to ECR as V2, schema 1	Pushed to ECR as V2, schema 2	Pushed to ECR as OCI
V2, schema 1	No translation required	Translated to V2, schema 1	Translated to V2, schema 1
V2, schema 2	No translation available, client falls back to V2, schema 1	No translation required	Translated to V2, schema 2
OCI	No translation available	Translated to OCI	No translation required

Important

If you pull an image *by digest*, there is no translation available; your client must understand the image manifest format that is stored in Amazon ECR. If you request a Docker Image Manifest V2 Schema 2 image by digest on a Docker 1.9 or older client, the image pull fails. For more information, see Registry compatibility in the Docker documentation.

However, in this example, if you request the same image *by tag*, Amazon ECR translates the image manifest into a format that the client can understand and the image pull succeeds.

Using Amazon ECR Images with Amazon ECS

You can use your ECR images with Amazon ECS, but you need to satisfy some prerequisites:

- Your container instances must be using at least version 1.7.0 of the Amazon ECS container agent. The latest version of the Amazon ECS–optimized AMI supports ECR images in task definitions. For more information, including the latest Amazon ECS–optimized AMI IDs, see Amazon ECS Container Agent Versions in the *Amazon Elastic Container Service Developer Guide.*

- The Amazon ECS container instance role (`ecsInstanceRole`) that you use with your container instances must possess the following IAM policy permissions for Amazon ECR.

```
 1  {
 2      "Version": "2012-10-17",
 3      "Statement": [
 4          {
 5              "Effect": "Allow",
 6              "Action": [
 7                  "ecr:BatchCheckLayerAvailability",
 8                  "ecr:BatchGetImage",
 9                  "ecr:GetDownloadUrlForLayer",
10                  "ecr:GetAuthorizationToken"
11              ],
12              "Resource": "*"
13          }
14      ]
15  }
```

  If you use the `AmazonEC2ContainerServiceforEC2Role` managed policy for your container instances, then your role has the proper permissions. To check that your role supports Amazon ECR, see Amazon ECS Container Instance IAM Role in the *Amazon Elastic Container Service Developer Guide.*

- In your ECS task definitions, make sure that you are using the full `registry/repository:tag` naming for your ECR images. For example, `aws_account_id.dkr.ecr.region.amazonaws.com``/my-web-app: latest`.

Deleting an Image

If you are done using an image, you can delete it from your repository. You can delete an image using the AWS Management Console, or the AWS CLI.

Note

If you are done with a repository, you can delete the entire repository and all of the images within it. For more information, see Deleting a Repository.

To delete an image with the AWS Management Console

1. Open the Amazon ECS console at https://console.aws.amazon.com/ecs/.

2. From the navigation bar, choose the region that contains the image to delete.

3. In the navigation pane, choose **Repositories**.

4. On the **Repositories** page, choose the repository that contains the image to delete.

5. On the **All repositories:** *repository_name* page, select the box to the left of the images to delete and choose **Delete**.

6. In the **Delete image(s)** dialog box, verify that the selected images should be deleted and choose **Delete**.

To delete an image with the AWS CLI

1. List the images in your repository so that you can identify them by image tag or digest.

```
1 aws ecr list-images --repository-name my-repo
```

2. (Optional) Delete any unwanted tags for the image by specifying the tag of the image you want to delete.
   Note
   When you delete the last tag for an image, the image is deleted.

```
1 aws ecr batch-delete-image --repository-name my-repo --image-ids imageTag=latest
```

3. Delete the image by specifying the digest of the image to delete. **Note**
   When you delete an image by referencing its digest, the image and all of its tags are deleted.

```
1 aws ecr batch-delete-image --repository-name my-repo --image-ids imageDigest=sha256:4
  f70ef7a4d29e8c0c302b13e25962d8f7a0bd304c7c2c1a9d6fa3e9de6bf552d
```

Amazon Linux Container Image

The Amazon Linux container image is built from the same software components that are included in the Amazon Linux AMI, and it is available for use in any environment as a base image for Docker workloads. If you are already using the Amazon Linux AMI for applications in Amazon EC2, then you can easily containerize your applications with the Amazon Linux container image.

You can use the Amazon Linux container image in your local development environment and then push your application to the AWS cloud using Amazon ECS. For more information, see Using Amazon ECR Images with Amazon ECS.

The Amazon Linux container image is available in Amazon ECR and on Docker Hub. Support for the Amazon Linux container image can be found by visiting the AWS developer forums.

To pull the Amazon Linux container image from Amazon ECR

1. Authenticate your Docker client to the Amazon Linux container image Amazon ECR registry. Authentication tokens are valid for 12 hours. For more information, see Registry Authentication. Specify the region that you would like to pull the image from (if you are unsure, the `us-west-2` region used in the command below is fine). If you do not use the `us-west-2` region for the following command, be sure to change the region in the subsequent commands and image tags. **Note**
The get-login command is available in the AWS CLI starting with version 1.9.15; however, we recommend version 1.11.91 or later for recent versions of Docker (17.06 or later). For more information, see Installing the AWS Command Line Interface in the *AWS Command Line Interface User Guide*.

```
1 aws ecr get-login --region us-west-2 --registry-ids 137112412989 --no-include-email
```

Example output:

```
1 docker login -u AWS -p password https://137112412989.dkr.ecr.us-west-2.amazonaws.com
```

Important
If you receive an `Unknown options: --no-include-email` error, install the latest version of the AWS CLI. For more information, see Installing the AWS Command Line Interface in the *AWS Command Line Interface User Guide*.

The resulting output is a docker login command that you use to authenticate your Docker client to the Amazon Linux container image Amazon ECR registry.

1. Copy and paste the docker login command into a terminal to authenticate your Docker CLI to the registry.
Important
When you execute this docker login command, the command string can be visible to other users on your system in a process list (ps -e) display. Because the docker login command contains authentication credentials, there is a risk that other users on your system could view them this way and use them to gain push and pull access to your repositories. If you are not on a secure system, you should consider this risk and log in interactively by omitting the `-p password` option, and then entering the password when prompted.

2. (Optional) You can list the images within the Amazon Linux repository with the aws ecr list-images command. The `latest` tag always corresponds with the latest Amazon Linux container image that is available.

```
1 aws ecr list-images --region us-west-2 --registry-id 137112412989 --repository-name
   amazonlinux
```

3. Pull the Amazon Linux container image using the docker pull command.

```
1 docker pull 137112412989.dkr.ecr.us-west-2.amazonaws.com/amazonlinux:latest
```

4. (Optional) Run the container locally.

```
1 docker run -it 137112412989.dkr.ecr.us-west-2.amazonaws.com/amazonlinux:latest /bin/bash
```

To pull the Amazon Linux container image from Docker Hub

1. Pull the Amazon Linux container image using the docker pull command.

```
1 docker pull amazonlinux
```

2. (Optional) Run the container locally.

```
1 docker run -it amazonlinux:latest /bin/bash
```

Amazon ECR Lifecycle Policies

Amazon ECR lifecycle policies enable you to specify the lifecycle management of images in a repository. A lifecycle policy is a set of one or more rules, where each rule defines an action for Amazon ECR. The actions apply to images that contain tags prefixed with the given strings. This allows the automation of cleaning up unused images, for example expiring images based on age or count. You should expect that after creating a lifecycle policy the affected images will be expired within 24 hours.

Topics

- Lifecycle Policy Template
- Lifecycle Policy Parameters
- Lifecycle Policy Evaluation Rules
- Creating a Lifecycle Policy Preview
- Creating a Lifecycle Policy
- Examples of Lifecycle Policies

Lifecycle Policy Template

The contents of your lifecycle policy is evaluated before being associated with a repository. The following is the JSON syntax template for the lifecycle policy. For lifecycle policy examples, see Examples of Lifecycle Policies.

```
 1  {
 2      "rules": [
 3          {
 4              "rulePriority": "integer",
 5              "description": string,
 6              "selection": {
 7                  "tagStatus": "tagged"|"untagged",
 8                  "tagPrefixList": list<string>,
 9                  "countType": "imageCountMoreThan"|"sinceImagePushed",
10                  "countUnit": "integer",
11                  "countNumber": "integer"
12              },
13              "action": {
14                  "type": "expire"
15              }
16          }
17      ]
18  }
```

Note
The `tagPrefixList` parameter is only used if `tagStatus` is `tagged`. The `countUnit` parameter is only used if `countType` is `sinceImagePushed`. The `countNumber` parameter is only used if `countType` is set to `imageCountMoreThan`.

Lifecycle Policy Parameters

Lifecycle policies are split into the following parts.

Topics

- Rule Priority
- Description
- Tag Status

- Tag Prefix List
- Count Type
- Count Unit
- Count Number
- Action

Rule Priority

rulePriority
Type: integer
Required: yes
When you add rules to a lifecycle policy, you must give it a unique rulePriority. Values do not need to be sequential across rules in a policy.

Description

description
Type: string
Required: no
The description is an optional field that can be used to describe the purpose of a rule within a lifecycle policy.

Tag Status

tagStatus
Type: string
Required: yes
This field determines whether the lifecycle policy rule you are adding specifies a tag for an image. Acceptable options are tagged or untagged. If you specify tagged, then you must also specify a tagPrefixList as well. If you specify untagged, then you must omit the tagPrefixList.

Tag Prefix List

tagPrefixList
Type: list[string]
Required: yes, only if tagStatus is set to tagged
This parameter is only used if you specified "tagStatus": "tagged". You must specify a comma-separated list of image tag prefixes on which to take action with your lifecycle policy. For example, if your images are tagged as prod, prod1, prod2, and so on, you would use the tag prefix prod to specify all of them. If you specify multiple tags, only images with all specified tags are selected.

Count Type

countType
Type: string
Required: yes
When you create a lifecycle policy, you specify a count type to apply to the images. If countType is set to imageCountMoreThan, you also specify countNumber to create a rule that sets a limit on the number of images that exist in your repository. If countType is set to sinceImagePushed, you also specify countUnit and countNumber to specify a time limit on the images that exist in your repository.

Count Unit

countUnit
Type: string
Required: yes, only if countType is set to sinceImagePushed
When you create a lifecycle policy, you specify a count unit of days to indicate that as the unit of time, in addition to countNumber, which is the number of days.

Count Number

countNumber
Type: integer
Required: yes
When you create a lifecycle policy, you specify a count number. If the countType used is imageCountMoreThan, then the value is the maximum number of images that you want to retain in your repository. If the countType used is sinceImagePushed, then the value is the maximum age limit for your images.

Action

type
Type: string
Required: yes
When you create a lifecycle policy, you specify an action type. The supported value is expire.

Lifecycle Policy Evaluation Rules

The lifecycle policy evaluator is responsible for parsing the plaintext JSON and applying it to the images in the specified repository. The following rules should be noted when creating a lifecycle policy:

- An image is expired by exactly one or zero rules.
- An image that matches the tagging requirements of a rule cannot be expired by a rule with a lower priority.
- Rules can never mark images matched by higher priority rules, but can still view them as if they haven't been expired.
- The set of rules must contain a unique set of tag prefixes.
- Only one rule is allowed to select untagged images.
- Expiration is always ordered by pushed_at_time, and always expires older images before newer ones.
- When using the tagPrefixList, an image is successfully matched if *all* of the tags in the tagPrefixList are matched against any of the image's tags.
- With countType = imageCountMoreThan, images are sorted from youngest to oldest based on pushed_at_time and then all images greater than the specified count are expired.
- With countType = sinceImagePushed, all images whose pushed_at_time is older than the specified number of days based on countNumber are expired.

Creating a Lifecycle Policy Preview

A lifecycle policy preview allows you to see the impact of a lifecycle policy on an image repository before you execute it. The following procedure shows you how to create a lifecycle policy preview using the console.

Setting up a lifecycle policy preview using the console

1. Open the Amazon ECS console at https://console.aws.amazon.com/ecs/.

2. From the navigation bar, choose the region that contains the repository on which to perform a lifecycle policy preview.

3. In the navigation pane, choose **Repositories** and select a repository.

4. On the **All repositories:** *repository_name* page, choose **Dry-Run Lifecycle Rules, Add**.

5. Enter the following details for your lifecycle policy rule:

    1. For **Rule Priority**, type a number for the rule priority.

    2. For **Rule Description**, type a description for the lifecycle policy rule.

    3. For **Image Status**, choose either **Tagged** or **Untagged**.

    4. If you specified Tagged for **Image Status**, then for **Tag Prefix List**, you can optionally specify a list of image tags on which to take action with your lifecycle policy. If you specified Untagged, this field must be empty.

    5. For **Match criteria**, choose values for **Count Type**, **Count Number**, and **Count Unit** (if applicable).

6. Choose **Save**

7. Create additional lifecycle policy rules by repeating steps 5–7.

8. To run the lifecycle policy preview, choose **Save and preview results**.

9. Under **Preview Image Results**, review the impact of your lifecycle policy preview.

10. If you are satisfied with the preview results, choose **Apply as lifecycle policy** to create a lifecycle policy with the specified rules.

Note

You should expect that after creating a lifecycle policy the affected images will be expired within 24 hours.

Creating a Lifecycle Policy

A lifecycle policy allows you to create a set of rules that expire unused repository images. The following procedure shows you how to create a lifecycle policy using the console. You should expect that after creating a lifecycle policy the affected images will be expired within 24 hours.

Setting up a lifecycle policy using the AWS CLI

1. Obtain the ID for the repository for which to create the lifecycle policy:

```
1 aws ecr describe-repositories
```

2. Create a lifecycle policy:

```
1 aws ecr put-lifecycle-policy [--registry-id <string>] --repository-name <string> --policy-
    text <string>
```

Setting up a lifecycle policy preview using the console

1. Open the Amazon ECS console at https://console.aws.amazon.com/ecs/.

2. From the navigation bar, choose the region that contains the repository on which to perform a lifecycle policy preview.

3. In the navigation pane, choose **Repositories**.

4. On the **Repositories** page, choose the repository on which to perform a lifecycle policy preview.

5. On the **All repositories:** *repository_name* page, choose **Lifecycle Policy, Add**.

6. Enter the following details for your lifecycle policy rule:

    1. For **Rule Priority**, type a number for the rule priority.

    2. For **Rule Description**, type a description for the lifecycle policy rule.

    3. For **Image Status**, choose either **Tagged** or **Untagged**.

    4. If you specified `Tagged` for **Image Status**, for **Tag Prefix List**, you can optionally specify a list of image tags on which to take action with your lifecycle policy. If you specified `Untagged`, this field must be empty.

    5. For **Match criteria**, choose values for **Count Type**, **Count Number**, and **Count Unit** (if applicable).

7. Choose **Apply as lifecycle policy. Note**
   If you choose **Dry Run**, it creates a lifecycle policy preview.

Examples of Lifecycle Policies

The following are example lifecycle policies, showing the syntax.

Topics

- Filtering on Image Age
- Filtering on Image Count
- Filtering on Multiple Rules
- Filtering on Multiple Tags in a Single Rule

Filtering on Image Age

The following shows the lifecycle policy syntax for a policy that expires untagged images older than 14 days:

```
1  {
2      "rules": [
3          {
4              "rulePriority": 1,
5              "description": "Expire images older than 14 days",
6              "selection": {
7                  "tagStatus": "untagged",
8                  "countType": "sinceImagePushed",
9                  "countUnit": "days",
10                 "countNumber": 14
11             },
12             "action": {
13                 "type": "expire"
14             }
15         }
16     ]
17 }
```

Filtering on Image Count

The following shows the lifecycle policy syntax for a policy that keeps only one untagged image and expires all others:

```
1  {
2      "rules": [
3          {
4              "rulePriority": 1,
5              "description": "Keep only one untagged image, expire all others",
6              "selection": {
7                  "tagStatus": "untagged",
8                  "countType": "imageCountMoreThan",
9                  "countNumber": 1
10             },
11             "action": {
12                 "type": "expire"
13             }
14         }
15     ]
16 }
```

Filtering on Multiple Rules

The following examples use multiple rules in a lifecycle policy. An example repository and lifecycle policy are given along with an explanation of the outcome.

Example A

Repository contents:

- Image A, Taglist: ["beta-1", "prod-1"], Pushed: 10 days ago
- Image B, Taglist: ["beta-2", "prod-2"], Pushed: 9 days ago
- Image C, Taglist: ["beta-3"], Pushed: 8 days ago

Lifecycle policy text:

```
 1  {
 2      "rules": [
 3          {
 4              "rulePriority": 1,
 5              "description": "Rule 1",
 6              "selection": {
 7                  "tagStatus": "tagged",
 8                  "tagPrefixList": ["prod"],
 9                  "countType": "imageCountMoreThan",
10                  "countNumber": 1
11              },
12              "action": {
13                  "type": "expire"
14              }
15          },
16          {
17              "rulePriority": 2,
18              "description": "Rule 2",
19              "selection": {
20                  "tagStatus": "tagged",
21                  "tagPrefixList": ["beta"],
22                  "countType": "imageCountMoreThan",
23                  "countNumber": 1
24              },
25              "action": {
26                  "type": "expire"
27              }
28          }
29      ]
30  }
```

The logic of this lifecycle policy would be:

- Rule 1 identifies images tagged with prefix `prod`. It should mark images, starting with the oldest, until there is one or fewer images remaining that match. It marks Image A for expiration.
- Rule 2 identifies images tagged with prefix `beta`. It should mark images, starting with the oldest, until there is one or fewer images remaining that match. It marks both Image A and Image B for expiration. However, Image A has already been seen by Rule 1 and if Image B were expired it would violate Rule 1 and thus is skipped.
- Result: Image A is expired.

Example B

This is the same repository as the previous example but the rule priority order is changed to illustrate the outcome.

Repository contents:

- Image A, Taglist: ["beta-1", "prod-1"], Pushed: 10 days ago
- Image B, Taglist: ["beta-2", "prod-2"], Pushed: 9 days ago
- Image C, Taglist: ["beta-3"], Pushed: 8 days ago

Lifecycle policy text:

```
1  {
2      "rules": [
3          {
4              "rulePriority": 1,
5              "description": "Rule 1",
6              "selection": {
7                  "tagStatus": "tagged",
8                  "tagPrefixList": ["beta"],
9                  "countType": "imageCountMoreThan",
10                 "countNumber": 1
11             },
12             "action": {
13                 "type": "expire"
14             }
15         },
16         {
17             "rulePriority": 2,
18             "description": "Rule 2",
19             "selection": {
20                 "tagStatus": "tagged",
21                 "tagPrefixList": ["prod"],
22                 "countType": "imageCountMoreThan",
23                 "countNumber": 1
24             },
25             "action": {
26                 "type": "expire"
27             }
28         }
29     ]
30 }
```

The logic of this lifecycle policy would be:

- Rule 1 identifies images tagged with `beta`. It should mark images, starting with the oldest, until there is one or fewer images remaining that match. It sees all three images and would mark Image A and Image B for expiration.
- Rule 2 identifies images tagged with `prod`. It should mark images, starting with the oldest, until there is one or fewer images remaining that match. It would see no images because all available images were already seen by Rule 1 and thus would mark no additional images.
- Result: Images A and B are expired.

Filtering on Multiple Tags in a Single Rule

The following lifecycle policy examples specify multiple tag prefixes in a single rule. An example repository and lifecycle policy are given along with an explanation of the outcome.

Example A

When multiple tag prefixes are specified on a single rule, images must match all listed tag prefixes.

Repository contents:

- Image A, Taglist: ["alpha-1"], Pushed: 12 days ago
- Image B, Taglist: ["beta-1"], Pushed: 11 days ago
- Image C, Taglist: ["alpha-2", "beta-2"], Pushed: 10 days ago
- Image D, Taglist: ["alpha-3"], Pushed: 4 days ago
- Image E, Taglist: ["beta-3"], Pushed: 3 days ago
- Image F, Taglist: ["alpha-4", "beta-4"], Pushed: 2 days ago

```
 1  {
 2      "rules": [
 3          {
 4              "rulePriority": 1,
 5              "description": "Rule 1",
 6              "selection": {
 7                  "tagStatus": "tagged",
 8                  "tagPrefixList": ["alpha", "beta"],
 9                  "countType": "sinceImagePushed",
10                  "countNumber": 5,
11                  "countUnit": "days"
12              },
13              "action": {
14                  "type": "expire"
15              }
16          }
17      ]
18  }
```

The logic of this lifecycle policy would be:

- Rule 1 identifies images tagged with `alpha` and `beta`. It sees images C and F. It should mark images that are older than five days, which would be Image C.
- Result: Image C is expired.

Example B

The following example illustrates that tags are not exclusive.

Repository contents:

- Image A, Taglist: ["alpha-1", "beta-1", "gamma-1"], Pushed: 10 days ago
- Image B, Taglist: ["alpha-2", "beta-2"], Pushed: 9 days ago
- Image C, Taglist: ["alpha-3", "beta-3", "gamma-2"], Pushed: 8 days ago

```
 1  {
 2      "rules": [
 3          {
 4              "rulePriority": 1,
```

```
 5          "description": "Rule 1",
 6          "selection": {
 7              "tagStatus": "tagged",
 8              "tagPrefixList": ["alpha", "beta"],
 9              "countType": "imageCountMoreThan",
10              "countNumber": 1
11          },
12          "action": {
13              "type": "expire"
14          }
15      }
16    ]
17 }
```

The logic of this lifecycle policy would be:

- Rule 1 identifies images tagged with `alpha` and `beta`. It sees all images. It should mark images, starting with the oldest, until there is one or fewer images remaining that match. It marks image A and B for expiration.
- Result: Images A and B are expired.

Amazon ECR IAM Policies and Roles

By default, IAM users don't have permission to create or modify Amazon ECR resources, or perform tasks using the Amazon ECR API. (This means that they also can't do so using the Amazon ECR console or the AWS CLI.) To allow IAM users to create or modify resources and perform tasks, you must create IAM policies that grant IAM users permission to use the specific resources and API operations they'll need, and then attach those policies to the IAM users or groups that require those permissions.

When you attach a policy to a user or group of users, it allows or denies the users permission to perform the specified tasks on the specified resources. For more information, see Permissions and Policies and Managing IAM Policies in the *IAM User Guide*.

Likewise, Amazon ECS container instances make calls to the Amazon ECR APIs on your behalf (to pull Docker images that are used in Amazon ECS task definitions), so they need to authenticate with your credentials. This authentication is accomplished by creating an IAM role for your container instances and associating that role with your container instances when you launch them. For more information, see Amazon ECS Container Instance IAM Role in the *Amazon Elastic Container Service Developer Guide*. For more information about IAM roles, see IAM Roles in the *IAM User Guide*.

Getting Started

An IAM policy must grant or deny permission to use one or more Amazon ECR operations. It must also specify the resources that can be used with the operation, which can be all resources, or in some cases, specific resources. The policy can also include conditions that you apply to the resource.

Amazon ECR partially supports resource-level permissions. This means that for some Amazon ECS API operations, you cannot specify which resource a user is allowed to work with for that operation; instead, you have to allow users to work with all resources for that operation.

Topics

- Policy Structure
- Amazon ECR Managed Policies
- Supported Resource-Level Permissions for Amazon ECR API Actions
- Creating Amazon ECR IAM Policies

Policy Structure

The following topics explain the structure of an IAM policy.

Topics

- Policy Syntax
- Actions for Amazon ECR
- Amazon Resource Names for Amazon ECR
- Condition Keys for Amazon ECR
- Checking that Users Have the Required Permissions

Policy Syntax

An IAM policy is a JSON document that consists of one or more statements. Each statement is structured as follows:

```
1  {
2    "Statement":[{
3      "Effect":"effect",
4      "Action":"action",
5      "Resource":"arn",
6      "Condition":{
7        "condition":{
8          "key":"value"
9          }
10       }
11     }
12   ]
13 }
```

There are various elements that make up a statement:

- **Effect:** The *effect* can be `Allow` or `Deny`. By default, IAM users don't have permission to use resources and API operations, so all requests are denied. An explicit allow overrides the default. An explicit deny overrides any allows.
- **Action**: The *action* is the specific API operation for which you are granting or denying permission. To learn about specifying *action*, see Actions for Amazon ECR.
- **Resource**: The resource that's affected by the action. Some Amazon ECR API operations allow you to include specific resources in your policy that can be created or modified by the operation. To specify a resource in the statement, you need to use its Amazon Resource Name (ARN). For more information about specifying the *arn* value, see Amazon Resource Names for Amazon ECR. For more information about which API operations support which ARNs, see Supported Resource-Level Permissions for Amazon ECR API Actions. If the API operation does not support ARNs, use the * (asterisk) wildcard to specify that all resources can be affected by the operation.
- **Condition**: Conditions are optional and can control when your policy will be in effect. For more information about specifying conditions for Amazon ECR, see Condition Keys for Amazon ECR.

Actions for Amazon ECR

In an IAM policy statement, you can specify any API operation from any service that supports IAM. For Amazon ECR, use the following prefix with the name of the API operation: `ecr:`. For example: `ecr:CreateRepository` and `ecr:DeleteRepository`.

To specify multiple operations in a single statement, separate them with commas as follows:

```
1 "Action": ["ecr:action1", "ecr:action2"]
```

You can also specify multiple operations using wildcards. For example, you can specify all operations whose name begins with the word "Delete" as follows:

```
1 "Action": "ecr:Delete*"
```

To specify all Amazon ECR API operations, use the * (asterisk) wildcard as follows:

```
1 "Action": "ecr:*"
```

For a list of Amazon ECR operations, see Actions in the *Amazon Elastic Container Registry API Reference*.

Amazon Resource Names for Amazon ECR

Each IAM policy statement applies to the resources that you specify using their ARNs.

Important
Currently, not all API actions support individual ARNs; we'll add support for additional API actions and ARNs for additional Amazon ECR resources later. For information about which ARNs you can use with which Amazon ECR API operations, see Supported Resource-Level Permissions for Amazon ECR API Actions.

An ARN has the following general syntax:

```
1 arn:aws:[service]:[region]:[account]:resourceType/resourcePath
```

service
The service (for example, `ecr`).

region
The region for the resource (for example, `us-east-1`).

account
The AWS account ID, with no hyphens (for example, `123456789012`).

resourceType
The type of resource (for example, `instance`).

resourcePath
A path that identifies the resource. You can use the * (asterisk) wildcard in your paths.

For example, you can indicate a specific repository (`my-repo`) in your statement using its ARN as follows:

```
1 "Resource": "arn:aws:ecr:us-east-1:123456789012:repository/my-repo"
```

You can also specify all repositories that belong to a specific account by using the * wildcard as follows:

```
1 "Resource": "arn:aws:ecr:us-east-1:123456789012:repository/*"
```

To specify all resources, or if a specific API operation does not support ARNs, use the * wildcard in the `Resource` element as follows:

```
1 "Resource": "*"
```

The following table describes the ARNs for each type of resource used by the Amazon ECR API operations.

Resource Type	ARN
All Amazon ECR resources	arn:aws:ecr:*
All Amazon ECR resources owned by the specified account in the specified region	arn:aws:ecr:*region*:*account*:*
Repository	arn:aws:ecr:*region*:*account*:repository/*repository-name*

Many Amazon ECR API operations accept multiple resources. To specify multiple resources in a single statement, separate their ARNs with commas, as follows:

```
1  "Resource": ["arn1", "arn2"]
```

For more information, see Amazon Resource Names (ARN) and AWS Service Namespaces in the *Amazon Web Services General Reference*.

Condition Keys for Amazon ECR

In a policy statement, you can optionally specify conditions that control when it is in effect. Each condition contains one or more key-value pairs. Condition keys are not case-sensitive. We've defined AWS-wide condition keys, plus additional service-specific condition keys.

If you specify multiple conditions, or multiple keys in a single condition, we evaluate them using a logical AND operation. If you specify a single condition with multiple values for one key, we evaluate the condition using a logical OR operation. For permission to be granted, all conditions must be met.

You can also use placeholders when you specify conditions. For more information, see Policy Variables in the *IAM User Guide*.

Amazon ECR implements the AWS-wide condition keys (see Available Keys),.

For example repository policy statements for Amazon ECR, see Amazon ECR Repository Policies.

Checking that Users Have the Required Permissions

After you've created an IAM policy, we recommend that you check whether it grants users the permissions to use the particular API operations and resources they need before you put the policy into production.

First, create an IAM user for testing purposes, and then attach the IAM policy that you created to the test user. Then, make a request as the test user. You can make test requests in the console or with the AWS CLI.

Note
You can also test your policies with the IAM Policy Simulator. For more information about the policy simulator, see Working with the IAM Policy Simulator in the *IAM User Guide*.

If the action that you are testing creates or modifies a resource, you should make the request using the `DryRun` parameter (or run the AWS CLI command with the `--dry-run` option). In this case, the call completes the authorization check, but does not complete the operation. For example, you can check whether the user can terminate a particular instance without actually terminating it. If the test user has the required permissions, the request returns `DryRunOperation`; otherwise, it returns `UnauthorizedOperation`.

If the policy doesn't grant the user the permissions that you expected, or is overly permissive, you can adjust the policy as needed and retest until you get the desired results.

Important
It can take several minutes for policy changes to propagate before they take effect. Therefore, we recommend that you allow five minutes to pass before you test your policy updates.

If an authorization check fails, the request returns an encoded message with diagnostic information. You can decode the message using the `DecodeAuthorizationMessage` action. For more information, see DecodeAuthorizationMessage in the *AWS Security Token Service API Reference*, and decode-authorization-message in the *AWS CLI Command Reference*.

Amazon ECR Managed Policies

Amazon ECR provides several managed policies that you can attach to IAM users or EC2 instances that allow differing levels of control over Amazon ECR resources and API operations. You can apply these policies directly, or you can use them as starting points for creating your own policies. For more information about each API operation mentioned in these policies, see Actions in the *Amazon Elastic Container Registry API Reference*.

Topics

- AmazonEC2ContainerRegistryFullAccess
- AmazonEC2ContainerRegistryPowerUser
- AmazonEC2ContainerRegistryReadOnly

AmazonEC2ContainerRegistryFullAccess

This managed policy allows full administrator access to Amazon ECR.

```
1  {
2    "Version": "2012-10-17",
3    "Statement": [
4      {
5        "Effect": "Allow",
6        "Action": [
7          "ecr:*"
8        ],
9        "Resource": "*"
10     }
11   ]
12 }
```

AmazonEC2ContainerRegistryPowerUser

This managed policy allows power user access to Amazon ECR, which allows read and write access to repositories, but does not allow users to delete repositories or change the policy documents applied to them.

```
1  {
2      "Version": "2012-10-17",
3      "Statement": [{
4          "Effect": "Allow",
5          "Action": [
6              "ecr:GetAuthorizationToken",
7              "ecr:BatchCheckLayerAvailability",
8              "ecr:GetDownloadUrlForLayer",
9              "ecr:GetRepositoryPolicy",
10             "ecr:DescribeRepositories",
11             "ecr:ListImages",
12             "ecr:DescribeImages",
13             "ecr:BatchGetImage",
14             "ecr:InitiateLayerUpload",
15             "ecr:UploadLayerPart",
16             "ecr:CompleteLayerUpload",
17             "ecr:PutImage"
18         ],
19         "Resource": "*"
```

```
20      }]
21  }
```

AmazonEC2ContainerRegistryReadOnly

This managed policy allows read-only access to Amazon ECR, such as the ability to list repositories and the images within the repositories, and also to pull images from Amazon ECR with the Docker CLI.

```
1  {
2      "Version": "2012-10-17",
3      "Statement": [{
4          "Effect": "Allow",
5          "Action": [
6              "ecr:GetAuthorizationToken",
7              "ecr:BatchCheckLayerAvailability",
8              "ecr:GetDownloadUrlForLayer",
9              "ecr:GetRepositoryPolicy",
10             "ecr:DescribeRepositories",
11             "ecr:ListImages",
12             "ecr:DescribeImages",
13             "ecr:BatchGetImage"
14         ],
15         "Resource": "*"
16     }]
17  }
```

Supported Resource-Level Permissions for Amazon ECR API Actions

Resource-level permissions refers to the ability to specify which resources users are allowed to perform actions on. Amazon ECR has partial support for resource-level permissions. This means that for certain Amazon ECR operations, you can control when users are allowed to use those operations based on conditions that have to be fulfilled, or specific resources that users are allowed to use.

The following table describes the Amazon ECR API operations that currently support resource-level permissions, as well as the supported resources and resource ARNs for each.

For a list of Amazon ECR operations, see Actions in the *Amazon Elastic Container Registry API Reference*.

Important
If an Amazon ECR API operation is not listed in this table, then it does not support resource-level permissions. If an API operation does not support resource-level permissions, you can grant users permission to use the operation, but you have to specify the * (asterisk) wildcard for the resource element of your policy statement.

API action	Resource	
BatchCheckLayerAvailability	Repository	arn:aws:ecr:*region*:*account*:repository/*my-repo*
BatchDeleteImage	Repository	arn:aws:ecr:*region*:*account*:repository/*my-repo*
BatchGetImage	Repository	arn:aws:ecr:*region*:*account*:repository/*my-repo*
CompleteLayerUpload	Repository	arn:aws:ecr:*region*:*account*:repository/*my-repo*
DeleteLifecyclePolicy	Repository	arn:aws:ecr:*region*:*account*:repository/*my-repo*
DeleteRepository	Repository	arn:aws:ecr:*region*:*account*:repository/*my-repo*
DeleteRepositoryPolicy	Repository	arn:aws:ecr:*region*:*account*:repository/*my-repo*
DescribeImages	Repository	arn:aws:ecr:*region*:*account*:repository/*my-repo*
DescribeRepositories	Repository	arn:aws:ecr:*region*:*account*:repository/*my-repo*
GetDownloadUrlForLayer	Repository	arn:aws:ecr:*region*:*account*:repository/*my-repo*
GetLifecyclePolicy	Repository	arn:aws:ecr:*region*:*account*:repository/*my-repo*
GetLifecyclePolicyPreview	Repository	arn:aws:ecr:*region*:*account*:repository/*my-repo*
GetRepositoryPolicy	Repository	arn:aws:ecr:*region*:*account*:repository/*my-repo*
InitiateLayerUpload	Repository	arn:aws:ecr:*region*:*account*:repository/*my-repo*
ListImages	Repository	arn:aws:ecr:*region*:*account*:repository/*my-repo*
PutImage	Repository	arn:aws:ecr:*region*:*account*:repository/*my-repo*
PutLifecyclePolicy	Repository	arn:aws:ecr:*region*:*account*:repository/*my-repo*
SetRepositoryPolicy	Repository	arn:aws:ecr:*region*:*account*:repository/*my-repo*

API action	Resource	
StartLifecyclePolicyPreview	Repository	arn:aws:ecr:*region*:*account*:repository/*my-repo*
UploadLayerPart	Repository	arn:aws:ecr:*region*:*account*:repository/*my-repo*

Creating Amazon ECR IAM Policies

You can create specific IAM policies to restrict the calls and resources that users in your account have access to, and then attach those policies to IAM users.

When you attach a policy to a user or group of users, it allows or denies the users permission to perform the specified tasks on the specified resources. For more general information about IAM policies, see Permissions and Policies in the *IAM User Guide*. For more information about managing and creating custom IAM policies, see Managing IAM Policies.

To create an IAM policy for a user

1. Open the IAM console at https://console.aws.amazon.com/iam/.

2. In the navigation pane, choose **Policies, Create Policy**.

3. In the **Create Policy** section, choose **Select** next to **Create Your Own Policy**.

4. For **Policy Name**, type your own unique name, such as `AmazonECRUserPolicy`.

5. For **Policy Document**, paste the policy to apply to the user. You can use the Amazon ECR Managed Policies as a starting point to create your own more or less restrictive IAM policies to use with Amazon ECR.

6. Choose **Create Policy** to finish.

To attach an IAM policy to a user

1. Open the IAM console at https://console.aws.amazon.com/iam/.

2. In the navigation pane, choose **Users** and then choose the user to attach the policy to.

3. Choose **Permissions, Add permissions**.

4. In the **Grant permissions** section, choose **Attach existing policies directly**.

5. Select the custom policy that you created in the previous procedure and choose **Next: Review**.

6. Review your details and choose **Add permissions** to finish.

Using the AWS CLI with Amazon ECR

The following steps will help you install the AWS CLI and then log in to Amazon ECR, create an image repository, push an image to that repository, and perform other common scenarios in Amazon ECR with the AWS CLI.

The AWS Command Line Interface (CLI) is a unified tool to manage your AWS services. With just one tool to download and configure, you can control multiple AWS services from the command line and automate them through scripts. For more information on the AWS CLI, see http://aws.amazon.com/cli/.

For more information on the other tools available for managing your AWS resources, including the different AWS SDKs, IDE toolkits, and the Windows PowerShell command line tools, see http://aws.amazon.com/tools/.

Topics

- Step 1: Authenticate Docker to your Default Registry
- Step 2: Get a Docker Image
- Step 3: Create a Repository
- Step 4: Push an Image to Amazon ECR
- Step 5: Pull an Image from Amazon ECR
- Step 6: Delete an Image
- Step 7: Delete a Repository

Step 1: Authenticate Docker to your Default Registry

After you have installed and configured the AWS CLI, you can authenticate the Docker CLI to your default registry so that the docker command can push and pull images with Amazon ECR. The AWS CLI provides a get-login command to simplify the authentication process.

To authenticate Docker to an Amazon ECR registry with get-login Note
The get-login command is available in the AWS CLI starting with version 1.9.15; however, we recommend version 1.11.91 or later for recent versions of Docker (17.06 or later). You can check your AWS CLI version with the aws --version command.

1. Run the aws ecr get-login command. The example below is for the default registry associated with the account making the request. To access other account registries, use the `--registry-ids aws_account_id` option. For more information, see get-login in the *AWS CLI Command Reference*.

```
1 aws ecr get-login --no-include-email
```

Output:

```
1 docker login -u AWS -p password https://aws_account_id.dkr.ecr.us-east-1.amazonaws.com
```

Important
If you receive an `Unknown options: --no-include-email` error, install the latest version of the AWS CLI. For more information, see Installing the AWS Command Line Interface in the *AWS Command Line Interface User Guide*.

The resulting output is a docker login command that you use to authenticate your Docker client to your Amazon ECR registry.

1. Copy and paste the docker login command into a terminal to authenticate your Docker CLI to the registry. This command provides an authorization token that is valid for the specified registry for 12 hours. **Note** If you are using Windows PowerShell, copying and pasting long strings like this does not work. Use the following command instead.

```
1 Invoke-Expression -Command (aws ecr get-login --no-include-email)
```

Important

When you execute this docker login command, the command string can be visible to other users on your system in a process list (ps -e) display. Because the docker login command contains authentication credentials, there is a risk that other users on your system could view them this way and use them to gain push and pull access to your repositories. If you are not on a secure system, you should consider this risk and log in interactively by omitting the -p password option, and then entering the password when prompted.

Step 2: Get a Docker Image

Before you can push an image to Amazon ECR, you need to have one to push. If you do not already have an image to use, you can create one by following the steps in Docker Basics for Amazon ECR, or you can simply pull an image from Docker Hub that you would like to have in your Amazon ECR registry. To pull the ubuntu:trusty image from Docker hub to your local system, run the following command:

```
1 $ docker pull ubuntu:trusty
2 trusty: Pulling from library/ubuntu
3 0a85502c06c9: Pull complete
4 0998bf8fb9e9: Pull complete
5 a6785352b25c: Pull complete
6 e9ae3c220b23: Pull complete
7 Digest: sha256:3cb273da02362a6e667b54f6cf907edd5255c706f9de279c97cfccc7c6988124
8 Status: Downloaded newer image for ubuntu:trusty
```

Step 3: Create a Repository

Now that you have an image to push to Amazon ECR, you need to create a repository to hold it. In this example, you create a repository called ubuntu to which you later push the ubuntu:trusty image. To create a repository, run the following command:

```
1 $ aws ecr create-repository --repository-name ubuntu
2 {
3     "repository": {
4         "registryId": "111122223333",
5         "repositoryName": "ubuntu",
6         "repositoryArn": "arn:aws:ecr:us-east-1:111122223333:repository/ubuntu"
7     }
8 }
```

Step 4: Push an Image to Amazon ECR

Now you can push your image to the Amazon ECR repository you created in the previous section. You use the docker CLI to push images, but there are a few prerequisites that must be satisfied for this to work properly:

- The minimum version of docker is installed: 1.7
- The Amazon ECR authorization token has been configured with docker login.
- The Amazon ECR repository exists and the user has access to push to the repository.

After those prerequisites are met, you can push your image to your newly created repository in the default registry for your account.

To tag and push an image to Amazon ECR

1. List the images you have stored locally to identify the image to tag and push.

```
1 $ docker images
2 REPOSITORY            TAG           IMAGE ID          CREATED         VIRTUAL
     SIZE
3 ubuntu               trusty        e9ae3c220b23      3 weeks ago     187.9 MB
```

2. Tag the image to push to your repository.

```
1 $ docker tag ubuntu:trusty aws_account_id.dkr.ecr.us-east-1.amazonaws.com/ubuntu:trusty
```

3. Push the image.

```
1 $ docker push aws_account_id.dkr.ecr.us-east-1.amazonaws.com/ubuntu:trusty
2 The push refers to a repository [aws_account_id.dkr.ecr.us-east-1.amazonaws.com/ubuntu] (
     len: 1)
3 e9ae3c220b23: Pushed
4 a6785352b25c: Pushed
5 0998bf8fb9e9: Pushed
6 0a85502c06c9: Pushed
7 trusty: digest: sha256:215d7e4121b30157d8839e81c4e0912606fca105775bb0636b95aed25f52c89b
     size: 6774
```

Step 5: Pull an Image from Amazon ECR

After your image has been pushed to your Amazon ECR repository, you can pull it from other locations. We will use the docker CLI to pull images, but there are a few prerequisites that must be satisfied for this to work properly:

- The minimum version of docker is installed: 1.7
- The Amazon ECR authorization token has been configured with docker login.
- The Amazon ECR repository exists and the user has access to pull from the repository.

After those prerequisites are met, you can pull your image. To pull your example image from Amazon ECR, run the following command:

```
1 $ docker pull aws_account_id.dkr.ecr.us-east-1.amazonaws.com/ubuntu:trusty
2 trusty: Pulling from ubuntu
3 0a85502c06c9: Pull complete
4 0998bf8fb9e9: Pull complete
5 a6785352b25c: Pull complete
6 e9ae3c220b23: Pull complete
7 Digest: sha256:215d7e4121b30157d8839e81c4e0912606fca105775bb0636b95aed25f52c89b
8 Status: Downloaded newer image for aws_account_id.dkr.ecr.us-east-1.amazonaws.com/ubuntu:trusty
```

Step 6: Delete an Image

If you decide that you no longer need or want an image in one of your repositories, you can delete it with the batch-delete-image command. To delete an image, you must specify the repository that it is in and either a imageTag or imageDigest value for the image. The example below deletes an image in the ubuntu repository with the image tag trusty.

```
1 $ aws ecr batch-delete-image --repository-name ubuntu --image-ids imageTag=trusty
2 {
3     "failures": [],
4     "imageIds": [
5         {
```

```
6          "imageTag": "trusty",
7          "imageDigest": "sha256:215
              d7e4121b30157d8839e81c4e0912606fca105775bb0636b95aed25f52c89b"
8      }
9    ]
10 }
```

Step 7: Delete a Repository

If you decide that you no longer need or want an entire repository of images, you can delete the repository. By default, you cannot delete a repository that contains images; however, the `--force` flag allows this. To delete a repository that contains images (and all the images within it), run the following command:

```
1  $ aws ecr delete-repository --repository-name ubuntu --force
2  {
3      "repository": {
4          "registryId": "aws_account_id",
5          "repositoryName": "ubuntu",
6          "repositoryArn": "arn:aws:ecr:us-east-1:aws_account_id:repository/ubuntu",
7          "createdAt": 1457671643.0,
8          "repositoryUri": "aws_account_id.dkr.ecr.us-east-1.amazonaws.com/ubuntu"
9      }
10 }
```

Amazon ECR Service Limits

The following table provides the default limits for Amazon ECR for an AWS account which can be changed. For more information, see AWS Service Limits in the *Amazon Web Services General Reference.*

Resource	Default Limit
Maximum number of repositories per account	1,000
Maximum number of images per repository	1,000
Maximum http://docs.aws.amazon.com/AmazonECR/latest/APIReference/API_GetAuthorizationToken.html API transactions per second, per account, per region	20 sustained, with the ability to burst up to 200 *

* In each region, each account receives a bucket that can store up to 200 http://docs.aws.amazon.com/AmazonECR/latest/APIReference/API_GetAuthorizationToken.html credits. These credits are replenished at a rate of 20 per second. If your bucket has 200 credits, you could achieve 200 http://docs.aws.amazon.com/AmazonECR/latest/APIReference/API_GetAuthorizationToken.html API transactions per second for one second, and then sustain 20 transactions per second indefinitely.

The following table provides other limitations for Amazon ECR and Docker images that cannot be changed.

Note
The layer part information mentioned in the table below is only applicable to customers who are calling the Amazon ECR APIs directly to initiate multipart uploads for image push operations (we expect this to be very rare).
We recommend that you use the docker CLI to pull, tag, and push images.

Resource	Default Limit
Maximum number of layers per image	127 (this is the current Docker limit)
Maximum number of tags per image	100
Maximum layer size **	10,000 MiB
Maximum layer part size	10 MiB
Minimum layer part size	5 MiB (except the final layer part in an upload)
Maximum number of layer parts	1,000

** The maximum layer size listed here is calculated by multiplying the maximum layer part size (10 MiB) by the maximum number of layer parts (1,000).

Logging Amazon ECR API Calls By Using AWS CloudTrail

Amazon ECR is integrated with CloudTrail, a service that captures all of the API calls made by or on behalf of Amazon ECR in your AWS account and delivers the log files to an Amazon S3 bucket that you specify. CloudTrail captures API calls from the Amazon ECR console or from the Amazon ECR API. Using the information collected by CloudTrail, you can determine what request was made to Amazon ECR, the source IP address from which the request was made, who made the request, when it was made, and so on. To learn more about CloudTrail, including how to configure and enable it, see the http://docs.aws.amazon.com/awscloudtrail/latest/userguide/.

Amazon ECR Information in CloudTrail

When CloudTrail logging is enabled in your AWS account, API calls made to Amazon ECR actions are tracked in log files. Amazon ECR records are written together with other AWS service records in a log file. CloudTrail determines when to create and write to a new file based on a time period and file size.

All of the Amazon ECR actions are logged by CloudTrail and are documented in the Amazon Elastic Container Registry API Reference. For example, calls to the **GetAuthorizationToken**, **CreateRepository** and **SetRepositoryPolicy** operations generate entries in the CloudTrail log files.

Every log entry contains information about who generated the request. The user identity information in the log helps you determine whether the request was made with root or IAM user credentials, with temporary security credentials for a role or federated user, or by another AWS service. For more information, see the **userIdentity** field in the CloudTrail Event Reference.

You can store your log files in your bucket for as long as you want, but you can also define Amazon S3 lifecycle rules to archive or delete log files automatically. By default, your log files are encrypted by using Amazon S3 server-side encryption (SSE).

You can choose to have CloudTrail publish Amazon SNS notifications when new log files are delivered if you want to take quick action upon log file delivery. For more information, see Configuring Amazon SNS Notifications.

You can also aggregate Amazon ECR log files from multiple AWS regions and multiple AWS accounts into a single S3 bucket. For more information, see Aggregating CloudTrail Log Files to a Single Amazon S3 Bucket.

Understanding Amazon ECR Log File Entries

CloudTrail log files can contain one or more log entries where each entry is made up of multiple JSON-formatted events. A log entry represents a single request from any source and includes information about the requested action, any parameters, the date and time of the action, and so on. The log entries are not guaranteed to be in any particular order. That is, they are not an ordered stack trace of the public API calls.

Amazon ECR Troubleshooting

This chapter helps you find diagnostic information for Amazon ECR, and provides troubleshooting steps for common issues and error messages.

Topics

- Enabling Docker Debug Output
- Enabling AWS CloudTrail
- Optimizing Performance for Amazon ECR
- Troubleshooting Errors with Docker Commands When Using Amazon ECR
- Troubleshooting Amazon ECR Error Messages

Enabling Docker Debug Output

To begin debugging any Docker-related issue, you should start by enabling Docker debugging output on the Docker daemon running on your host instances. For more information about enabling Docker debugging if you are using images pulled from Amazon ECR on Amazon ECS container instances, see Enabling Docker Debug Output in the *Amazon Elastic Container Service Developer Guide*.

Enabling AWS CloudTrail

Additional information about errors returned by Amazon ECR can be discovered by enabling AWS CloudTrail, which is a service that records AWS calls for your AWS account and delivers log files to an Amazon S3 bucket. By using information collected by CloudTrail, you can determine what requests were successfully made to AWS services, who made the request, when it was made, and so on. To learn more about CloudTrail, including how to turn it on and find your log files, see the AWS CloudTrail User Guide. For more information on using CloudTrail with Amazon ECR, see Logging Amazon ECR API Calls By Using AWS CloudTrail.

Optimizing Performance for Amazon ECR

The following section provides recommendations on settings and strategies that can be used to optimize performance when using Amazon ECR.

Use Docker 1.10 and above to take advantage of simultaneous layer uploads
Docker images are composed of layers, which are intermediate build stages of the image. Each line in a Dockerfile results in the creation of a new layer. When you use Docker 1.10 and above, Docker defaults to pushing as many layers as possible as simultaneous uploads to Amazon ECR, resulting in faster upload times.

Use a smaller base image
The default images available through Docker Hub may contain many dependencies that your application doesn't require. Consider using a smaller image created and maintained by others in the Docker community, or build your own base image using Docker's minimal scratch image. For more information, see Create a base image in the Docker documentation.

Place the dependencies that change the least earlier in your Dockerfile
Docker caches layers, which speeds up build times. If nothing on a layer has changed since the last build, Docker uses the cached version instead of rebuilding the layer. However, each layer is dependent on the layers that came before it. If a layer changes, Docker recompiles not only that layer, but any layers that come after that layer as well.
To minimize the time required to rebuild a Docker file and to re-upload layers, consider placing the dependencies that change the least frequently earlier in your Dockerfile, and place rapidly changing dependencies (such as your application's source code) later in the stack.

Chain commands to avoid unnecessary file storage

Intermediate files created on a layer remain a part of that layer even if they are deleted in a subsequent layer. Consider the following example:

```
1 WORKDIR /tmp
2 RUN wget http://example.com/software.tar.gz
3 RUN wget tar -xvf software.tar.gz
4 RUN mv software/binary /opt/bin/myapp
5 RUN rm software.tar.gz
```

In this example, the layers created by the first and second RUN commands contain the original .tar.gz file and all of its unzipped contents, even though the .tar.gz file is deleted by the fourth RUN command. These commands can be chained together into a single RUN statement to ensure that these unnecessary files aren't part of the final Docker image:

```
1 WORKDIR /tmp
2 RUN wget http://example.com/software.tar.gz &&\
3     wget tar -xvf software.tar.gz &&\
4     mv software/binary /opt/bin/myapp &&\
5     rm software.tar.gz
```

Use the closest regional endpoint

You can reduce latency in pulling images from Amazon ECR by ensuring that you are using the regional endpoint closest to where your application is running. If your application is running on an Amazon EC2 instance, you can use the following shell code to obtain the region from the Availability Zone of the instance:

```
1 REGION=$(curl -s http://169.254.169.254/latest/meta-data/placement/availability-zone |\
2     sed -n 's/\(\d*\)[a-zA-Z]*$/\1/p')
```

The region can be passed to AWS CLI commands using the --region parameter, or set as the default region for a profile using the aws configure command. You can also set the region when making calls using the AWS SDK. For more information, see the documentation for the SDK for your specific programming language.

Troubleshooting Errors with Docker Commands When Using Amazon ECR

Topics

- Error: "Filesystem Verification Failed" or "404: Image Not Found" When Pulling an Image From an Amazon ECR Repository
- Error: "Filesystem Layer Verification Failed" When Pulling Images from Amazon ECR
- HTTP 403 Errors or "no basic auth credentials" Error When Pushing to Repository

In some cases, running a Docker command against Amazon ECR may result in an error message. Some common error messages and potential solutions are explained below.

Error: "Filesystem Verification Failed" or "404: Image Not Found" When Pulling an Image From an Amazon ECR Repository

You may receive the error `Filesystem verification failed` when using the docker pull command to pull an image from an Amazon ECR repository with Docker 1.9 or above, or the error `404: Image not found` when using Docker versions prior to 1.9.

Some possible reasons and their explanations are given below.

The local disk is full
If the local disk on which you're running the docker pull command is full, then the SHA-1 hash that is calculated on the locally downloaded file may be different than the SHA-1 hash calculated by Amazon ECR. Check that your local disk has enough remaining free space to store the Docker image you are pulling. You can also delete old images to make room for new ones. Use the docker images command to see a list of all locally downloaded Docker images, along with their sizes.

Client cannot connect to the remote repository due to network error
Calls to an Amazon ECR repository require a functioning connection to the Internet. Verify your network settings, and verify that other tools and applications can access resources on the Internet. If you are running the docker pull command on an Amazon EC2 instance in a private subnet, verify that your private subnet has a route to the Internet through a network address translation (NAT) server or through a managed NAT gateway. Currently, calls to an Amazon ECR repository also require network access through your corporate firewall to Amazon Simple Storage Service (Amazon S3). If your organization uses firewall software or a NAT device that white lists allowed service endpoints, ensure that the Amazon S3 service endpoints for your current region are included in the whitelist.
If you are using Docker behind an HTTP proxy, you can configure Docker with the appropriate proxy settings. For more information, see HTTP proxy in the Docker documentation.

Error: "Filesystem Layer Verification Failed" When Pulling Images from Amazon ECR

You may receive the error `image image-name not found` when pulling images using the docker pull command. If you inspect the Docker logs, you may see an error like the following:

```
1 filesystem layer verification failed for digest sha256:2b96f...
```

This error indicates that one or more of the layers for your image has failed to download. Some possible reasons and their explanations are given below.

You are using an older version of Docker
This error can occur in a small percentage of cases when using a Docker version less than 1.10. Upgrade your Docker client to 1.10 or greater.

Your client has encountered a network or disk error
A full disk or a network issue may prevent one or more layers from downloading, as discussed earlier about the `Filesystem verification failed` message,. Follow the recommendations above to ensure that your filesystem is not full, and that you have enabled access to Amazon S3 from within your network.

HTTP 403 Errors or "no basic auth credentials" Error When Pushing to Repository

There are times when you may receive an HTTP 403 (Forbidden) error, or the error message `no basic auth credentials` from the docker push command, even if you have successfully authenticated to Docker using the aws ecr get-login command. The following are some known causes of this issue:

You have authenticated to a different region
Authentication requests are tied to specific regions, and cannot be used across regions. For example, if you obtain an authorization token from US West (Oregon), you cannot use it to authenticate against your repositories in US East (N. Virginia). To resolve the issue, ensure that you are using the same region for both authentication and docker push command calls.

You have authenticated to push to a repository on the wrong AWS account
If you are using an IAM user from one AWS account, but you are attempting to push to a repository hosted in another account, you will need to explicitly specify the `--registry-ids` parameter when you call `aws ecr get-login`. Otherwise, you will by default get a Docker login command which only authorizes you to push to repositories on the same account that hosts your IAM user, not the account that hosts your repository. Always ensure that the repository URL in the response from `aws ecr get-login` matches the repository URL that you are pushing to, including the account ID portion of the URL.

Your token has expired
The default token expiration period for tokens obtained using the `GetAuthorizationToken` operation is 12 hours. However, if you use a temporary security credential mechanism such as multi-factor authentication (MFA) or AWS Security Token Service to authenticate and receive your token, the expiration period of the Amazon ECR authorization token is equal to the duration of these temporary security credentials. For example, if you call the aws ecr get-login command by assuming a role, the authorization token expires within 15 minutes to 1 hour, depending on the settings you use when calling the aws sts assume-role command.

Bug in `wincred` credential manager
Some versions of Docker for Windows use a credential manager called `wincred`, which does not properly handle the Docker login command produced by aws ecr get-login (for more information, see https://github.com/docker/docker/issues/22910). You can run the Docker login command that is output, but when you try to push or pull images, those commands will fail. You can work around this bug by removing the `https://` scheme from the registry argument in the Docker login command that is output from aws ecr get-login. An example Docker login command without the HTTPS scheme is shown below.

```
1 docker login -u AWS -p <password> -e none <aws_account_id>.dkr.ecr.<region>.amazonaws.com
```

Troubleshooting Amazon ECR Error Messages

Topics

- Error: "Error Response from Daemon: Invalid Registry Endpoint" When Running aws ecr get-login
- HTTP 429: Too Many Requests or ThrottleException
- HTTP 403: "User [arn] is not authorized to perform [operation]"
- HTTP 404: "Repository Does Not Exist" Error

In some cases, an API call that you have triggered through the Amazon ECS console or the AWS CLI exits with an error message. Some common error messages and potential solutions are explained below.

Error: "Error Response from Daemon: Invalid Registry Endpoint" When Running aws ecr get-login

You may see the following error when running the aws ecr get-login command to obtain the login credentials for your Amazon ECR repository:

```
1  Error response from daemon: invalid registry endpoint
2      https://xxxxxxxxxxxx.dkr.ecr.us-east-1.amazonaws.com/v0/: unable to ping registry endpoint
3      https://xxxxxxxxxxxx.dkr.ecr.us-east-1.amazonaws.com/v0/
4  v2 ping attempt failed with error: Get https://xxxxxxxxxxxx.dkr.ecr.us-east-1.amazonaws.com/v2/:
5      dial tcp: lookup xxxxxxxxxxxx.dkr.ecr.us-east-1.amazonaws.com on 172.20.10.1:53:
6      read udp 172.20.10.1:53: i/o timeout
```

This error can occur on MacOS X and Windows systems that are running Docker Toolbox, Docker for Windows, or Docker for Mac. It is often caused when other applications alter the routes through the local gateway (192.168.0.1) through which the virtual machine must call to access the Amazon ECR service. If this error occurs when using Docker Toolbox, then it can often be resolved by restarting the Docker Machine environment, or rebooting the local client operating system. If this does not resolve the issue, use the docker-machine ssh command to log in to your container instance, and perform a DNS lookup on an external host to verify that you see the same results as you see on your local host. If the results differ, consult the documentation for Docker Toolbox to ensure that your Docker Machine environment is configured properly.

HTTP 429: Too Many Requests or ThrottleException

You may receive a `429: Too Many Requests` error or a `ThrottleException` error from one or more Amazon ECR commands or API calls. If you are using Docker tools in conjunction with Amazon ECR, then for Docker versions 1.12.0 and greater, you may see the error message `TOOMANYREQUESTS: Rate exceeded`. For versions of Docker below 1.12.0, you may see the error `Unknown: Rate exceeded`.

This indicates that you are calling a single endpoint in Amazon ECR repeatedly over a short interval, and that your requests are getting throttled. Throttling occurs when calls to a single endpoint from a single user exceed a certain threshold over a period of time.

Various API operations in Amazon ECR have different throttles.

For example, the throttle for the http://docs.aws.amazon.com/AmazonECR/latest/APIReference/API_ GetAuthorizationToken.html action is 20 transaction per second (TPS), with up to a 200 TPS burst allowed. In each region, each account receives a bucket that can store up to 200 `GetAuthorizationToken` credits. These credits are replenished at a rate of 20 per second. If your bucket has 200 credits, you could achieve 200 `GetAuthorizationToken` API transactions per second for one second, and then sustain 20 transactions per second indefinitely.

To handle throttling errors, implement a retry function with incremental backoff into your code. For more information, see Error Retries and Exponential Backoff in AWS in the Amazon Web Services General Reference.

HTTP 403: "User [arn] is not authorized to perform [operation]"

You may receive the following error when attempting to perform an action with Amazon ECR:

```
1  $ aws ecr get-login
2  A client error (AccessDeniedException) occurred when calling the GetAuthorizationToken operation
   :
3     User: arn:aws:iam::account-number:user/username is not authorized to perform:
4     ecr:GetAuthorizationToken on resource: *
```

This indicates that your user does not have permissions granted to use Amazon ECR, or that those permissions are not set up correctly. In particular, if you are performing actions against an Amazon ECR repository, verify that the user has been granted permissions to access that repository. For more information about creating and verifying permissions for Amazon ECR, see Amazon ECR IAM Policies and Roles.

HTTP 404: "Repository Does Not Exist" Error

If you specify a Docker Hub repository that does not currently exist, Docker Hub creates it automatically. With Amazon ECR, new repositories must be explicitly created before they can be used. This prevents new repositories from being created accidentally (for example, due to typos), and it also ensures that an appropriate security access policy is explicitly assigned to any new repositories. For more information about creating repositories, see Amazon ECR Repositories.

Document History

The following table describes the important changes to the documentation since the last release of Amazon ECR. We also update the documentation frequently to address the feedback that you send us.

- **Current API version:** 2015-09-21
- **Latest documentation update:** November 21, 2017

Feature	API Version	Description	Release Date
Amazon ECR Name Change	2015-09-21	Amazon Elastic Container Registry is renamed (previously Amazon EC2 Container Registry).	November 21, 2017
Lifecycle Policies	2015-09-21	Amazon ECR lifecycle policies enable you to specify the lifecycle management of images in a repository. For more information, see Amazon ECR Lifecycle Policies.	October 11, 2017
Amazon ECR support for Docker image manifest 2, schema 2	2015-09-21	Amazon ECR now supports Docker Image Manifest V2 Schema 2 (used with Docker version 1.10 and newer). For more information, see Container Image Manifest Formats.	January 27, 2017
Amazon ECR General Availability	2015-09-21	Amazon Elastic Container Registry (Amazon ECR) is a managed AWS Docker registry service that is secure, scalable, and reliable.	December 21, 2015

AWS Glossary

For the latest AWS terminology, see the AWS Glossary in the *AWS General Reference*.

www.ingramcontent.com/pod-product-compliance
Lightning Source LLC
LaVergne TN
LVHW082041050326
832904LV00005B/268